GLEAMS

FROM

THE SICK CHAMBER.

Memorial Thoughts of Consolation and Hope gathered from the Epistles of St. Peter.

(A BOOK ALONE FOR SUFFERERS.)

BY THE AUTHOR OF

"MORNING AND NIGHT WATCHES."

"Beloved, think it not strange concerning the fiery trial which is to try you, as though some strange thing happened unto you. But rejoice, inasmuch as ye are partakers of Christ's sufferings; that when His glory shall be revealed, ye may be glad also with exceeding joy."

St. Peter's First Epistle, iv. 12, 13

"A light that shineth in a dark place, until the day dawn, and the day star arise in your hearts."

St. Peter's Second Epistle, i. 19.

LONDON:

JAMES NISBET & CO., 21 BERNERS STREET.

MDCCCLXXXII.

Printed by Ballantyne, Hanson & Co.,
Edinburgh and London.

This Book

CAN BE DEDICATED TO

ONE ONLY.

The future is dark and the pilgrimage dreary:
    For " the strong staff is broken—the beautiful rod ; "
But rejoice in the rest HE has made for the weary,
    Where widowhood's pathway no more can be trod :
        " Sweet rest !—sweet rest !
    Sweet rest that remains for the people of God ! "

Though called thus to hang your mute harp on the willows,
    And to mourn for the loved one beneath the green sod ;
You can think of his song in the midst of the billows,
    As he passed through the channel of Jordan 'dryshod :'
        " Sweet rest !—sweet rest !
    Sweet rest that remains for the people of God ! "

PREFACE.

———o———

THE following pages had their birthnight at a prolonged sick-bed. They are now a voice from the sainted dead.

Any value they may have, therefore, arises from a close, sacred fellowship with suffering. They are solely for those called to this severe (in many respects severest) discipline. Others would have little patience for them. To these, indeed, the Volume would be quite out of place, unseasonable, and inappropriate; so that should it accidentally fall into their hands, let them at once lay it aside. It was said that there was a gate in the Temple of old, open only for mourners. There is such also for those habituated to days of pain and nights of weariness; and it is they alone (I may be forgiven the repetition), who are invited here to enter.

Without trenching on the inviolate sacredness of personal and family sorrow, it may be

b

well at once on the threshold, to state a little more specifically, the occasion of the themes dwelt upon in what follows.

There are two verses which may be described as the pivot upon which all the subsequent part of the Book turns. Without these indeed, it would have had no existence. They are inserted as one of the mottoes on the title-page; adapted also as a befitting close to each daily portion:—" *Beloved, think it not strange concerning the fiery trial which is to try you, as though some strange thing happened unto you: but rejoice, inasmuch as ye are partakers of Christ's sufferings ; that, when His glory shall be revealed, ye may be glad also with exceeding joy* " (1 Pet. iv. 12, 13). To the writer, this passage will always be like a bright meteor amid other stars irradiating the valley-gloom of suffering and death; or, to use St. Peter's own words, " a light shining in a dark place; " the pledge and harbinger of blessed " day-dawn " (2 Pet. i. 19).

One morning when seated by a couch of severe distress, the exclamation was made through increasing weakness, but with an ecstatic glow ever to be remembered :—" Oh, I cannot tell you how that one verse has strengthened me during the night. It has never left me. I never thought of the amazing consolation in it before. Often as I have read it, I never thought of suffering in that light. Wonderful! *partakers with Christ in His sufferings.* What a privilege! Well, it has given me great endurance. I hardly know how I could have passed through the night without it. But it has calmed and soothed me. I am sure it will be a strengthener to me all through. Oh! just to think, *honoured* to suffer with Christ! partaker with *Him,*—fellowship in *His* sufferings!"

That night, alas! stood not alone; there were very many " tossings to and fro until the dawning of the day" yet appointed. But the elevating and sustaining theme became subsequently quite a pillow for the aching head. That same day it was reverted to, more than once, to others as well as myself; and yet again with the recurring and ever-augmented pain of evening. I copy these words from the last note I had, written in pencil with a trembling hand. " *Last night I was in fearful pain ; but by God's grace I was able to endure it, and I pondered much the precious words. How it elevates and ennobles suffering—' Beloved, think it not strange . . . rather* REJOICE *in being made partaker' . . . &c. I can see it was all needed, and all will be well.*"

I had to leave next forenoon. Two days after, a telegram (it turned out of needless urgency) summoned me at midnight to the same bedside. The impossibility of reaching by the ordinary means necessitated a long drive. But the sky was gemmed with innumerable stars ; and, what never can be forgotten, it happened to afford the most favourable view of the remarkable comet of June (Friday 24th). Next morning had brought slightly revived strength, and with it the old theme of the "rejoicing in the fiery trial," and the wonderful participation in suffering with the Prince of sufferers. The bright firmament of the preceding night was referred to as a comforting parable, with the well-known, yet never commonplace illustration, of the stars of Christian promise coming out most luminously when the sun of health and prosperity had gone down. But over and above this, the farther thought suggested itself of the brilliant " meteor-verse " with its new trail of glory. Like its type in the heavens, it seemed for the time not only to pale, but really paled and eclipsed all its favourite compeers in the Bible galaxy. " And it came to pass, that when the sun went down and it was dark, behold . . . a burning lamp ! " (Gen. xv. 17).

While this one passage occupied so much thought and reflection, it naturally led to digging for new lodes in the same inspired mine. The rich and varied themes of both St. Peter's Epistles (specially the First) were now and again explored, and always with fresh interest and comfort. I confess I was myself never before adequately aware of how very full of solace and heart-cheer these two precious letters are. The writer of them might divide with Barnabas the honoured title of " Son of Consolation." To any one who devoutly ponders their contents, it will be seen that they are portions of the Word pre-eminently fitted for the chamber of sickness and suffering, and, when it pleases God, for the bed of death. To revert to nature's parable; they have the brilliance of the meteor, with all the enduring glory and lustre of the true constellation.

There appear to be three golden threads of Peace, Consolation, and Hope, specially running through these Epistles, or as they may rather be called, more in harmony with the name of this Book, three *Golden Gleams.* .

The First is, the light of lights; the central truth of all;—apart from which no other spiritual comfort or encouragement is possible;— *the precious Sacrifice and finished work of Jesus.* Not, as we shall find, expressed in the cold negations of modern theology, but the grand, old, undiluted verity of pardon and peace through the blood of the cross. Oh! how poor, in such an hour, is any hope compared to *this!* *

---

* Among other favourite themes in what follows, it will be found that one, oft recurred to, is "the upbuilding of Mercy's Temple," of which Believers are "the living stones" (1 Pet. ii. 5). But the reference was always unmistakable to a spiritual building having its foundation in the completed atonement of Christ.

The Second is, that which, as already explained, originated this little volume. First of all, the *privilege* (strange thus to speak of it!) —the *privilege of sanctified suffering.* And then, the utterly amazing privilege of *being made partakers with Christ in* His *sufferings,*—the identification of the believer with his dear Lord in His cross and agony. Let any one simply glance (particularly over the contents of the first Epistle) and see how, to the wide family of sufferers, the sufferings of the Great Master are continually held up to view. The thought is repeated and reiterated to disarm the sting of their own. " Christ *suffered* for us " (ii. 21). " Christ also hath once *suffered* " (iii. 18). " As Christ hath *suffered* " (iv. 1). " Partakers of Christ's sufferings " (iv. 13).*

Then, passing from this to the special calling and prerogative to share the Saviour's cross and drink His cup, Peter—now transfigured in his whole spiritual nature—never forgot the

* " He who dated his own faith from the sufferings of his Master, is never weary of holding up the suffering Form of the Lord before the eyes of his readers to comfort and stimulate them."—*Wiesinger*, quoted by Dean Alford, 'Greek Testament.'

last utterance of reponed love and forgiveness:
" What is that to thee? follow thou Me."* He
was, doubtless, as all Christ's people are, mightily
strengthened at the last for the endurance even
of bodily pain. What had once been said, with
rash impetuosity, by the two sons of Zebedee in
answer to Christ's words, " Are ye able to drink
of the cup that I shall drink of, and to be baptized with the baptism that I am baptized
with ? " he could now, by grace, utter in calm
serenity, " I *am* able " (Matt. xx. 21, 22).

The Third of these gleams of light is, " *The
glory that is to be revealed*": the crown rising
above the cross. He quickens His converts
by the elevating thought of 'the blessed hope,'
'the glorious appearing,' 'the day-dawn, and
day-star' (2 Pet. i. 19):—God, as a Father,
preparing, by His own loving though often
severe discipline, for the eternal Home,—the
inheritance incorruptible and undefiled, and
that fadeth not away (i. 4).

Thus, then, we have, if I can so with reverence express it, a glorious trinity of divine

* John xxi. 22. Peter had a like Passion with the Lord.
—*Tertullian.*

consolations, in these two rich repertories of promise.

The Blessedness of acceptance.

The Privilege of suffering.

The Assurance of glory.

Perhaps in one verse alone are all the three combined (1 Pet. v. 10). We may transpose the words thus—

" The God of all grace *by Christ Jesus.*"

" After that ye have *suffered awhile.*"

" Who hath called us unto *His Eternal glory.*"

One is forcibly reminded of the Saviour's own ever-memorable words—" I am *the Way,* and *the Truth,* and *the Life* " (John xiv. 6). The Way—the way of acceptance. The Truth —true and truthful to His purposes of wisdom and love in all His dealings. The Life—the Purchaser, Revealer, Bestower of ' Glory'— Life everlasting !

Such are the themes which, as rehearsed in the following pages, helped materially to cheer and solace the weary, suffering hours of one of God's dear children. The evidences of " peace and joy in believing," thus indirectly and faintly recalled, were no mere sudden parting beams, as life's sun was nearing the horizon; but rather, as many well know, the outcome and expression of a consecrated life. During the unusually lengthened watchings and the long silent intervals, necessitated, owing to extreme weakness and prostration, the writer felt he could not better or more congenially employ a portion at least of these hours (elsewhere also)—than in transcribing and expanding, in the first instance for the use and comfort of others, some mutual thoughts and reflections suggested by these Epistles; but it further occurred—specially as the sacred and privileged vigil was drawing to a close, that he might at the same time unobtrusively interweave these, with not a few hallowed recent memories; in this way rendering whatever might be penned, more suited and available for kindred sufferers than any mere series of meditations or reflections could be. It struck him, moreover, for the twofold object he had thus in view, that he might be forgiven adopting the somewhat novel treatment of casting combined fragments of thought and conversation in a letter-form—the form, indeed, in which one or two of them originally were. He feels, in moulding into this shape, the obvious disadvantage of introducing far more of personal element and statement than he could have desired, but which in the circumstances was unavoidable. Still more does he dislike appearing to assume the office of Instructor, when he was really and in truth all the while the instructed. He is responsible simply for the setting ; anything more precious is not his.

With this somewhat long statement to prevent misapprehension, he sends these snatches of Night-song forth on their lowly mission, with the hope and prayer, that by God's blessing they may help to impart needed strength to others who are subjected to similar " fiery trials,"—disclosing to them in the midst of the furnace " one like unto the Son of God." Or, if he may borrow a figure from a Minister of Consolation, his cherished desire will be fulfilled, should this unpretending Volume become a cloud to carry a few exhaled dew-drops of comfort to some thirsty land and pining sufferer. It is enough to say, that no greater privilege can be enjoyed by any human soul, than, directly or indirectly, to " speak a word in season to him that is weary." *

" As men live, so do men die." And it may well be added, as in this case, even when in God's mysterious providence the sun of life wades through very dark and heavy clouds of physical endurance, all the brighter are the gleams of light—golden bars—in the troubled western sky; the evidence at once of a radiance behind the clouds, and the pledge and prophecy of a more glorious rising. The words may be added, but thank God they apply to bodily sufferings and no more; for from the first to the last, faith was undimmed by so much as one passing shadow—" Deep calleth unto deep at the noise of Thy water-spouts: all Thy waves and Thy billows are gone over me. Yet the Lord will command His loving-kindness in the day-time, and in the night His song shall be with me, and my prayer unto the God

* There was little difficulty in adapting what follows (indeed they seemed naturally to fall into the arrangement), for a month's daily reading, in case of any sufferers being desirous thus to use them.

of my life. I will say unto God my rock, Why hast Thou forgotten me; why go I mourning because of the oppression of the enemy?....
Why art thou cast down, O my soul? and why art thou disquieted within me? hope thou in God: for I shall yet praise Him, who is the health of my countenance, and my God" (Ps. xlii. 7, 8, 9, 11).

That climax of Faith—Hope—VICTORY— was reached!

⁂ This note may be regarded as somewhat out of harmony with the rest of the Book, but the writer deems that a few words may be appropriately appended, regarding the contents of the two Epistles which occupy so special a place in what follows. Though on this, as it is well known, there are conflicting theories of no signification here—it is our belief that Peter was now in his old age, probably about the year 63, resident in Babylon; not the figurative Babylon (Rome), but in the old capital of Chaldea, ministering there to the 'diaspora,' the Jews of the dispersion. In the partition of Evangelical work at the first Council of Jerusalem by the Apostolic leaders, while the mission of his great (shall we say greater) Brother Paul was to the vast heathen world, "far hence unto the Gentiles,"—Peter's appropriated sphere was the "circumcision,"—to carry the glad tidings to the multitude of his brethren according to the flesh, the lost sheep of the house of Israel, scattered in these Eastern regions—the towns and cities of Asia Minor

and the countries watered by the Tigris and Euphrates. Of the latter, Babylon was the important centre.

The first Epistle, which had the priority in time, was written to such as were suffering from the "fiery trial" of persecution; doubtless, in the case of many, including those severe bodily sufferings to which he himself was served heir by his Lord, and which, as above noted, he endured unflinchingly in the closing hours of all. " The trial of their faith" is the key-note of the letter (i. 7).

The second Epistle seems to have been penned subsequently, in consequence, to him, of yet sadder "fiery trials," arising from defection in doctrine and disloyalty to the truth. But, whatever the peculiar characteristics and phases of these first-age tribulations may have been, the divine solaces and consolations remain the same to the wide, suffering family of God; nay, the special commission which Peter received from his Divine Master, seems, in these precious legacies of comfort, to have been in his own mind when he made his bequest, through them, to the holy Church throughout all the world — " When thou art converted, STRENGTHEN thy brethren."

CONTENTS.

—o—

The Sprinkling of the Blood of Jesus Christ.

MY DEAR ——

Much have I thought, since we parted, of your wonderful verse. But you were right. The opening clause in the 1st Epistle may well take the precedence of it and of all others. You might truly call that clause the " golden prop " on which hangs every promise of the present and every hope of the future. All other themes of consolation would be worthless without this —" *The sprinkling of the blood of Jesus Christ* " (1 Pet. i. 2).

It is surely interesting and remarkable, that just as we are on the threshold of these two precious Epistles, we should thus find their lintels sprinkled, so to speak, with the sacrificial blood! Your own Passover picture now hanging before me, with its impressive inscription " WHEN I SEE THE BLOOD I WILL PASS

A

OVER YOU," is an ever-present memorial of the old rite. The more one thinks of it, indeed, the more significant was that " sprinkling," occurring (or rather enjoined) just as the Hebrews were about to set out on " the great and terrible wilderness." A blessed way thus to commence the mighty march with all its unknown vicissitudes. Happy they (happy *you*) who begin the desert of trial, whatever its duration and its appointments may be, with your eye falling on no unfamiliar symbol; but that which has ever formed your "hope and joy and crown of rejoicing "—the blood of the " everlasting covenant "—the finished atoning work of " Christ our Passover sacrificed for us."

I think we are warranted in supposing that Peter's own past appears, every now and then, throughout these letters of his, in what might be called 'reflected lights!' It was as the Great Anti-type of the Paschal lamb—" the Lamb of God"—that he himself had Jesus, indirectly, first pointed out to him (John i. 29, 36). Here the blood of that Lamb " slain from the foundation of the world" is given as his first thought for the sufferers of his age. He feels as if he could not wait beyond the opening salutation to introduce the glorious truth upon which all his own hopes were founded, alike for time and for eternity.

Your present sufferings have been, happily, like these wilderness trials of Israel, all unforeseen. How often have you lately spoken of that merciful provision—"Ye know not what shall be on the morrow;" and of how graciously God screens from His people's view their coming afflictions. Yes, truly, were it otherwise, life's anticipated evils would mar all the gladness of its passing happiest hours. That bright April afternoon, only six weeks ago, when you had these forty village children to tea and games on the lawn, how little you dreamt of the sudden arrest of your many such pleasures, and what the morrow, and after-morrows, were to bring! Or, while occupied with —— in sowing your annual seeds and planting the gladiolus bulbs you fully expected to enjoy, how little thought had you that an inveterate ailment and couch of pain would render all impossible! Well is it for us to be able to say, regarding our every plan and purpose, great and little—

"Lead Thou me on :
I do not ask to see
The distant scene, one step enough for me."

Moses inquired no more about the desert journey after he had got the promise—" My presence shall go with thee, and I will give thee rest."

You might well say, though I put it in different words, that that "*sprinkling of the blood of Jesus Christ*" is a sure guarantee that God will not only love you *through* every suffering hour, but that even *in* the suffering He will deal most tenderly with you. " He that spared not His own Son !" After that pledge of His love there can be no superfluous spark in the fiery trial. I have not forgotten the fervour of last night's hymn. I know from —— it has long been one of the favourites you loved to repeat on many a bygone Sabbath's first waking:—

> " Oh for a heart to praise my God !
> A heart from sin set free ;
> A heart *besprinkled with the blood*
> *So freely shed for me !* "

Unexpectedly you have been called to encounter affliction and suffering in a form never before experienced by you. How unspeakably blessed (to close as I began) that you have not to face the trial of all trials—that of sin unforgiven, a Saviour unsought and unknown. Resting on the assurance, "And the blood of Jesus Christ His Son cleanseth from all sin," you can hear the cherished words, not with apprehension, but rather as if listening to the voice of some God-sent Angel of comfort—

" *Beloved, think it not strange concerning the fiery trial which is to try you, as though some strange thing happened unto you : but rejoice.*"

Suffering for a Season, if need be.

MY DEAR ——

I thankfully recall the clear and emphatic way you dwelt on the commencing thought about " the sprinkling of the blood of Jesus Christ." Be assured it is cheering and sustaining to others as well as to yourself, how simply, fully, without hesitation or qualification, you accept of this prime foundation-truth. When we parted, you translated all into the most familiar of lines, which must be ever cherished by you and me for another's sake—

"Nothing in my hands I bring,
Simply to Thy cross I cling."

We must take however, time about, St. Peter's themes of support. It is the privilege of SUFFERING which comes in turn to-day; and it is well that we selected his very first reference, occurring in the opening of the Epistle. I don't wonder at your liking for the three precious monosyllables which all poor afflicted ones cling to, as a specially tender message from their Father in Heaven; viz., that it is only "*if need be*" they are "*in heaviness through manifold temptations*" (1 Pet. i. 6). In other words, there is a divine *necessity* for your present "fiery trial." No drop in the cup can be spared. "I will correct thee in *measure*" (Jer. xxx. 11). He, tenderer and more loving than the tenderest earthly parent, tempers the fury of the flames, saying, "Thus far shalt thou go, and no farther." Happy for you, that with such confident trust in God, you can write over that severest hour of distress—"if need be." Over every future night of throbbing temples, and sleepless eyes—"if need be." Over every fresh thorn sent to buffet, over every heavier cross sent to carry—"if need be."

Your dear friend's "Desert Psalm" (cxiv.) we were just beginning to speak about, when pain interrupted. But it comes in appropriately here; for the leading thought in it is, *God guiding His people;* "the presence of the Lord" (ver. 7); the Pillar going before them night and day, without intermission, till needed no more on the other side of Jordan. These forty years between Egypt and Canaan were indeed one long miracle of Providence, — a record of Jehovah's protecting power and love, from the first dividing of the Red Sea to the final crossing of the border river :—"The sea saw it and fled, Jordan was driven back" (ver. 3). Then the closing verse seems so beautifully to sum up all the successive "*needs be*" of harassing wilderness discipline; transforming trials into mercies; Marahs followed only with more abundant Elims :—"the presence of the God of Jacob; which turned the rock into a standing water, the flint into a fountain of waters" (Ps. cxiv. 7, 8).

If this, as I know it is, be precisely your own experience, you may well trust HIM in the future, alike as to the *condition*, and the *limitation.*

"If need be"—"for a season." He will not permit the trial to go too far. He precedes His people indeed often now, as He did of old (taking the expression in a symbolic sense), in a pillar, either of *cloud* or of *fire:* " Clouds and darkness are round about Him!" "A fire goeth before Him!" But of them, as of His ancient Israel, it is still true: " He led them forth also by the *right* way." Not their own way, the way of their own choosing; but that of His selection, and therefore the best. " *This* also cometh from the Lord of Hosts," is a precious reassuring text for you to repose on. Knowing, believing, trusting, let Him speak to you to-day, even should it be out of the *cloudy* and *fiery* pillar, the words of His servant, but which are in deed and in truth His very own—

" *Beloved, think it not strange concerning the fiery trial which is to try you, as though some strange thing happened unto you; but rejoice.*"

The Incorruptible and Unfading Inheritance.

MY DEAR ——

We are brought in due order, to-day, to our third theme, THE COMING GLORY, the crown rising above the cross.

How delightful to think, and to *know*, that that time is most assuredly approaching, on which you so earnestly dwell—every suffering hour brings it nearer—when all this "needed," but it may be mysterious discipline shall be finally ended. In St. Peter's commencing words, it is quite a magnificent vista of glory which opens before you! He speaks of a "lively hope," and then tells to what that lively hope conducts :—" *To an inheritance incorruptible, and undefiled, and that fadeth not away, reserved in heaven for you, who are kept by the power of God through faith unto salvation*" (1 Pet. i. 4, 5). Or, as you yourself expressed it, with an emphasis I can never forget, "My flesh and my heart faileth; BUT God is the strength of my heart, and my portion *for ever*" (Ps. lxxiii. 26). Some one has spoken of the history of Joseph as the Old Testament type and picture of God's dealings with His people in every age, and under all dispensations; "THROUGH Suffering TO Glory." Thank God, you also have been brought to recognise the one as the appointed means to an everlasting end; that you are able not only to "think it not strange," but with such perfect calmness and trust to repeat Paul's great words: "I reckon that the sufferings of this present time are not worthy to be compared with the glory which shall be revealed in us." The "Bridge of Suffering" (is it George Herbert who calls it so?) will soon be crossed. It will be cut down behind you. Every memory of sad and sorrowful things will be banished and forgotten; angel-voices greeting you on the farther side with the welcome of that verse which has such music to all sufferers: "And there shall be no more death, neither sorrow, nor crying, neither shall there be any more pain; for the former things are passed away" (Rev. xxi. 4).

You remember, the other morning, how you hailed the gladsome return of light; welcoming with the words, "Weeping may endure for a night, but joy cometh in the morning." The better Morning is now breaking on you with its unfading glory. Yes, "*unfading.*" For this is the main feature in the words of to-day,—the permanent and enduring in contrast with the insecure and the temporary; incorruptible in contrast with corruptible; unfading in contrast with fading. Our suggestive comet with all its brilliancy will soon have melted from view in distant space. What perhaps is more apposite, this afternoon's rainbow, made out of transient shower-drops and a passing break of sunshine, has utterly passed away and left not a wreck behind. Type of the unenduring nature of earth's best and loveliest. But there is "a

Rainbow in sight like unto an emerald" (emblem of perpetuity), "round about the throne" (Rev. iv. 3). Gazing from your couch of suffering on that ' Bow without the cloud,' you can triumphantly say, "We look not at the things which are seen, but at the things which are not seen: for the things which are seen are temporal; but the things which are not seen are eternal" (2 Cor. iv. 18).

Oh how well worth "the heaviness through manifold temptations," and the sufferings " for a season," with so glorious a reversion! I confess it was very touching, indeed altogether at first saddening, to hear you speak of the things you loved most here, one after another, sensibly slipping from your grasp. But what if you are on the threshold—the borderland —of what can never perish? The verse in which you have so often joined on Sunday evenings had a peculiar significance sung to you when we last met—

" For ever with the Lord ! "

Until that glorious "day dawn," and that "daystar arise"——

"Beloved, think it not strange concerning the fiery trial which is to try you, as though some strange thing happened unto you: but rejoice, inasmuch as ye are partakers of Christ's sufferings; that, when His glory shall be revealed, ye may be glad also with exceeding joy."

Redeemed by the Lamb without blemish.

MY DEAR ——

I am back again in rotation to the great truth in which all our hopes centre. I think while you will like, for variety's sake, to alternate the three themes, we need not depart from the order in which they occur in the Epistles, but take them exactly as they evolve themselves in the Apostle's own mind.

It is surely another of your " golden sayings " which comes to us to-day. A former remark may be repeated, that Peter, in writing the verses, may again possibly have recalled the first sight and the first name of his beloved Master. Truly you might say, " what glorious words to live upon ! what glorious words to suffer upon ! what glorious words to die upon !" Just hear them once more, though so lately read together : " *Forasmuch as ye know that ye were not redeemed with corruptible things, such as silver and gold, . . . but with the precious blood of Christ, as of a lamb without blemish and without spot* " (1 Pet. i. 18, 19).

Redeemed by the precious blood of Christ! The work, the doing and dying of a sinless Saviour. In that beautiful passage of Revelation to which you so fondly turned the other night, where the sainted multitude above are spoken of as having " come out of great tribulation," it is not the tribulation which has brought them there. Suffering, of itself, never did and never could bring a soul to heaven. But "they have washed their robes and made them white *in the blood of the Lamb;* THEREFORE are they before the throne of God." While the very last words you quoted were those of their eternal song : " Unto Him that loved us, and washed us from our sins in His own blood."

I do not need to exhort *you*, for it has ever been with you the theme of all themes, the sun and centre of your spiritual firmament, to cling to the Saviour's absolutely perfect Work and vicarious Sacrifice. I liked the remark you made some time ago, which you had either heard or read (I think you said it was in a sermon of ——) about the obedience of Jesus; that even *before* He suffered on the cross He exclaimed, " I HAVE *finished* the work which Thou gavest Me to do." It became Him, in our room and stead, to fulfil all righteousness. That perfect obedience being rendered, the mighty work was further and fully consummated by the pouring out of His life's-blood. Thus alike He paid the penalty due to sin, and wrought out a perfect, everlasting righteousness. I do not know if I have rightly caught up your idea or made it clear; but at all events your meaning is very clear in the old familiar couplet you ended with, as having now a significance doubly real and doubly precious to you—

> " On Christ the solid Rock I stand,
> All other ground is sinking sand."

The " solid Rock," by the by, reminds me of what —— told me of a series of sermons

B

you heard last summer, on the texts of which your main comment was, " I can't forget ' Lead me to the Rock that is *higher than I.*' " You had no dream then of the " overwhelmed heart" with which the Psalmist introduces the words. But the prayer has been answered, and you never felt more firmly set than you now are on that Rock of Ages.

With such a sure foundation as this,—the glorious consciousness that the Redemption is complete, nothing to add, nothing to supplement,—let these murmuring waves of present suffering, as they break on the Rock, only show how secure thereon your footing is. Suffering such as yours is, *must*, indeed, be hard enough to bear; yet how harder far but for the assurance " safe in Christ." And if, under the divine teaching and discipline, it be the means of endearing *Him*, then

" *Beloved, think it not strange concerning the fiery trial which is to try you, as though some strange thing happened unto you: but rejoice.*"

Faith Tried by Fire.

My Dear ——

It is the note of tribulation to-day, the old dirge of *suffering*; "*The trial* (or as we read last night in the Revised Version, '*the proof*') *of your faith.*" God at times sees meet to test His children, as in your case, by no common ordeals, but "*by fire.*" He puts them into the furnace.

"Trials of faith" are of varied kinds. You spoke with thankfulness of being delivered from one—the saddest of all in times like this, when the very foundations of belief seem to tremble. When the storm unexpectedly comes, the moorings, sufficient for the unruffled sea, are strained to the utmost. Blessed, and much to be envied, are those, like yourself, who, for long happy years, have had all such questions finally resolved; whose hopes and beliefs have

been, and are, so securely anchored, that the
unlooked-for hurricane passes by you un-
scathed; rather, only, as I said in our last,
strengthens your hold of the Eternal Rock.

Or, Faith's trial may be not of an intellec-
tual, but of a moral and physical, kind: the
test required that of patience and submission
under severe chastisement; an unwavering confidence in the love, wisdom, and rectitude of
God, amid mysterious dealings. Just exactly
the experience which you told me you had
yourself for two long weeks to battle with.
How many feel exactly the same. "If the
Lord be with us, why should all this have be-
fallen us?" Why this sudden extinction of
hope? why this shadow on life's meridian
dial? Why, above all, should the very shadow
be deepened and intensified with the aggrava-
tion of sore suffering?

"Beloved, think it not strange concerning
the fiery trial *which* (in the preferable rendering of the Revised Version) *cometh upon you
to prove you,*" &c. Thanks be to God, this too

with you *has* been *proved;* and you can now
adhibit your testimony to Peter's, in the verse
at present before us, that faith, thus tested,
is " *much more precious than of gold which
perisheth though it be tried with fire* " (1 Pet.
i. 7). " Blessed," says his brother Apostle, " is
the man that endureth temptation (or trial),
for" (when he is so "tried" and stands the
searching ordeal) " he shall receive the Crown
of life, which the Lord hath promised to them
that love Him " (James i. 12).

We have spoken more than once of Peter's
personal experience mingling with many allu-
sions in his Epistles.   Perhaps when he wrote
thus of " the fiery trial" he did so with a tear
in his eye.   He surely could hardly help recalling, with a feeling of shame and humilia-
tion, how, when put to the proof, his own faith
sadly failed; the gold in the fining furnace
turning into dross and alloy.   But he was an
altered man since then: God had armed him
with a fresh supply of grace to meet fiercer
trial-hours.   The time was when he could

reply to Christ's test-questions only with a
hollow boast. Now all was different. Through
the same God-given grace may we not further
believe he was able too at his martyrdom to
say unfalteringly, "Why cannot I follow Thee
now? I will lay down my life for Thy
sake."

You have the same "God of all grace" to
deal with. And so has every member of the
family of suffering. May you continue—I cannot doubt it—to "glorify Him *in the fires.*"
St. Peter's prayer in this same Epistle you tell
me is your own: "That God in all things may
be glorified through Jesus Christ" (iv. 4).
Most soothing, surely, to feel, whatever your
sufferings have been or may be, that the Saviour
not only *appoints* them, but appoints them for
this great end. Nay, may I not add (I know you
do not fear the allusion) that the very words
He once used regarding His Apostle may come
from His lips of love with reference to your
present trial: "*This* spake *He, signifying by
what death He should glorify God*" (John xxi.

19). Though, moreover, you yourself may not be conscious of it, all this may take the shape of a message to those near and dear to you for their comfort and consolation in a similar hour, encouraging them also to " glorify God in the day of visitation." Give them this leaflet from the book of your experience—

" *Beloved, think it not strange concerning the fiery trial which is to try you, as though some strange thing happened unto you : but rejoice.*"

GLORY.

" Found unto Praise, and Honour, and Glory."

MY DEAR ——

We need not travel beyond yesterday's verse in search of the third theme in St. Peter's triplet.

Before doing so, will it be very much out of place, if I say, speaking of the trials of faith, how much struck I was with your own account of one of the *minor* kinds of these, and how it was you so successfully overcame it this past winter? Yes; the serious discouragements of your Sunday class, like many other such trials, were well worth enduring for the " proof" they led to. I shall not readily forget your pointing to the armchair at your bedside, and telling, as the true secret of success, the quarter of an hour's earnest pleading with God for a blessing each night before the meeting; its manifest bestowal; and that to an extent you never enjoyed before. Well, if such as this be not incentive and heart-cheer to many faint hearts among us, I know not what is.

But to return to our subject of to-day. The faith " tried with fire," emerging triumphant from the sevenfold-heated furnace, is "*found unto praise, and honour, and glory, at the appearing of Jesus Christ*" (1 Pet. i. 7). You remember what you said to me about 'the *Vessels of mercy*'? It would almost seem as if Peter were speaking of these Vessels coming forth refined and purified from the furnace, fitted for the heavenly Temple, and " for the Master's use." Their contents are here described. They are filled with " praise, and honour, and glory."

PRAISE.—The feeble, faltering tongue unable to sing now will sing then. It will praise God, first, for the bright parts of the journey. In your case these have been many. Let me say, too, that among the lifelong blessings you have to be grateful for, specially when we encounter so often the morbid moping of others, has been pre-eminently that of a thankful spirit. It evidently survives still. It was, to use a common phrase—"like you:" when —— began reading you a somewhat mournful hymn, your remark was, "Not that;" rather—

> "Oh for a heart to praise my God."

But it is "*trial*" that is also here said to be at last "found unto praise." Yes, strange as it may appear, such will doubtless be the case with the retrospect of your present seasons of darkness and disappointment—of sorrow and severe suffering. You will then at least recognise and adore in *all*, the sovereignty and faithfulness of God. I seem still to hear the closing verse and the appropriate tune with their many associations, that was so sweetly played to you last night, though you could only join in silence—

> "And when on earth I breathe no more
> The prayer, oft mixed with tears before,
> I'll sing upon a happier shore—
>   Thy will be done!"

HONOUR. —"Such honour have all His

saints." Honour, as His redeemed child.
Honoured *now* to be partaker with Christ in
His sufferings and cross; honoured *then* to be
partakers with Him in His triumph and crown.
" Them that honour Me," says God, " I will
honour." None would more sensitively shrink
than you, from the thought of any honour bestowed, still less merited, for feeble, mingled,
imperfect duty performd on earth. But neither
should you reject the comfort which such words
as these now suggest. " For God is not
unrighteous to forget your work and labour
of love which ye have showed toward His
name, in that ye have ministered to the saints
and do minister " (Heb. vi. 10). " If any man
serve Me, him will My Father honour." How
do I venture on such delicate ground as this?
Why, because I saw, two days ago, a tear in
your eye, which had its explanation in the
words, " Oh that I had done more than I
have done!" I remarked nothing at the time,
because it was quite evident you felt what you
said, and to have disputed the accuracy of

the self-reproach would have been out of place
and unkind. But I thought to myself, soon
after, that among the solaces, all of which
you so greatly need in your hour of weakness, why should not that one be spoken of
and thankfully included? Did not your Saviour, who never spoke a needless flattering
word, Himself utter it?—" Whosoever shall
give a cup of cold water to one of these little
ones in My name, verily I say unto you he
shall in no wise lose his reward." Yes—you
can well take in this gracious assurance. Few
are better warranted in humble gratitude to do
so. How many draughts of refreshment have
you given to *all:* encouraging words to the
children; cheering words to the old; faithful
words to young men in the battle of life and
treading the edge of the volcano; strengthening
words and generous deeds to the unaided and
desponding and unsuccessful; and a wealth
of little kindnesses to every one! Well, re-
prove me if you think I deserve it for calling
up such reminiscences; but I cannot help

drying that needless tear and smoothing your pillow with your great Master's own utterance : " Inasmuch as ye have done it unto one of the least of these My brethren, ye have done it unto Me." You say, any poor efforts you owe entirely to the grace and strength given you by Another. Undoubtedly so. Let us call them by the old words if you like : " precious fruits brought forth by *the Sun.*" But the fruits are there.

I have left myself no space to do more than mention the third theme—faith "*found unto* GLORY." Glory beyond what tongue can tell or heart conceive ; glory that will leave no room or space for so much as one memory of trial or suffering. Glory, a reflected glory, which, as dependent planets, His redeemed people get from that central Sun : " The glory which Thou gavest *Me*, I have given *them* " (John xvii. 22). How sublimely does St. Paul speak, alike of the name, honour, and destiny of the redeemed ; linking moreover, as here, the *suffering* with the *glory :* " And if children, then heirs; heirs of God, and joint-heirs with Christ; if so be that we suffer with Him, that we may be also glorified together."

Oh lift up your weary, suffering head, for this your Redemption draweth nigh ! Rejoicing in hope of the glory of God—

" Beloved, think it not strange concerning the fiery trial which is to try you, as though some strange thing happened unto you: but rejoice, inasmuch as ye are partakers of Christ's sufferings; that, when His glory shall be revealed, ye may be glad also with exceeding joy."

The Lively Hope.

My Dear ——

We must have a rehearsal to-day of one of your well-worn verses, I think I may add, one of your very favourite themes. For over and above, being itself in the truest sense a foundation-truth, it is one which very specially hallows suffering, brightens hope, takes the ' strangeness ' away from ' fiery trials,'—takes the sting away from death itself, and opens wide to us the gates of glory. " *Blessed be the God and Father of our Lord Jesus Christ, which according to His abundant mercy hath begotten us again unto a lively hope by the resurrection of Jesus Christ from the dead* " (1 Pet. i. 3). What a heaping of Gospel wealth and riches and comfort we have found here !

You are always unwilling to pass over the ever-gracious and welcome reference to

God as a *Father*—" the Father of our Lord
Jesus Christ," and in Him the Father of all
His covenant people. " My Father and your
Father; My God and your God." That word
seems at once to disarm fear, and inspire confidence and love. As you truly said, the divine
Fatherhood, in the only real meaning of the
term as applied to His own children, is one of
the truths we have to feel thankful for as having been brought more prominently out in the
Christian system in modern times; I may add
it has served to correct many false and un-
worthy views of the Great Being who " dealeth
with us as with sons." It is to sufferers like
yourself that that Name is specially endeared.
As a Father He is now correcting you. The
voice is a Father's voice, the rod is a Father's
rod. " My God, my Father!" is the opening note
—the keynote—of your dearly loved hymn,
which, by the by, much struck me the other
night where it speaks of " recalled loans." Is
not health (*your* health) one of these, quite as
much as friends ? It is a *Father* you address,

as He revokes the loan or lease of bodily vigour
He has hitherto bestowed—

> " If Thou shouldst call me to resign
> What once I prized, it ne'er was mine;
> I only yield Thee what is Thine:
> Thy will be done !"

It is not, however, in relation to suffering
that God the Father is here mentioned. That
we shall come to in other verses. But it is
rather in connection with *His abundant mercy
in Christ.* "Abundant mercy!" You were
speaking to me lately, indeed again and again,
of an impressive sermon on the grand upbuilding of the Temple of Mercy: "Mercy shall be
built up for ever." Here, alike is the founda-
tion-stone and the coping-stone of that divine
fabric, " *the resurrection of Jesus Christ from
the dead.*" It formed the proof and pledge of
a completed redemption, and a guarantee for
all spiritual blessings in Him:—" I am the
resurrection and the life. He that believeth in
Me, though he were dead, yet shall he live; and
whosoever liveth and believeth in Me shall

c

never die." But not only does this glorious doctrine, this glorious *fact*, attest a finished salvation; what to you must now form a truth of growing interest and blessedness, it is also the sure pledge of your own resurrection. In living union with the ever-living Redeemer, the corruptible shall yet put on incorruption, and the mortal immortality. That last Easter Sunday seems to have been to you one of the days memorable for comfort. There must have been much throughout the bright service to remind you of "Christ the first-fruits, afterward they that are Christ's at His coming." No wonder St. Peter speaks so ardently about it. None possibly could have had a more vivid impression of the Saviour's resurrection, as a sublime reality, than he. He was the first of the honoured Apostle-witnesses. Paul expressly tells of His risen Lord, "that He was seen (first) of Cephas, *then* of the twelve" (1 Cor. xv. 5). He surely must have had his own,—mingled doubtless, yet very wonderful, very reassuring memories of that first Christian

Sabbath. " The Lord hath risen indeed, *and hath appeared to Simon*" (Luke xxiv. 34). What! to Simon, after all his baseness and foul ingratitude ? Yes, and appeared doubtless, too, with nothing but a benediction. Can we wonder that when he writes about " the resurrection of Jesus Christ from the dead," he should use such phrases here as these?—"*Abundant mercy,*" " *A lively hope,*" " BLESSED *be God !* "

Take for your own comfort and the strengthening of your faith other kindred words of the Master Himself, which must have been also formerly listened to by St. Peter: " Verily, verily, I say unto you, The hour is coming in the which all that are in the graves shall hear the voice of the Son of God !" For that Advent-hour, with its unveiled mysteries, its explained Providences, its blissful reunions, its eternal fellowship and communion with a Living Lord, He has been, and now is, through much mysterious discipline, preparing you. The present is " not joyous but grievous." But let the words of a brother Apostle, like a rainbow of light, span the interval—" *When Christ who is your life shall appear, then shall ye also appear with Him in glory.*"   Oh, with that great Easter-day of the Church triumphant in prospect, is there not a strain of reviving music to you—a glorious " night-song" in the words—

" *Beloved, think it not strange concerning the fiery trial which is to try you, as though some strange thing happened unto you : but rejoice, inasmuch as ye are partakers of Christ's sufferings ; that, when His glory shall be revealed, ye may be glad also with exceeding joy.*"

The Sufferings of Christ.

MY DEAR ——

What a subject is this which to-day comes in order for our second topic, " *the sufferings of Christ* " *!* (1 Pet. i. 11).

None, in one sense, could know so much about these as Peter did. We saw that he claims for himself, in the last chapter of this Epistle, the special designation " a witness of the sufferings of Christ " (v. 1). He had been an habitual spectator of them during the three years of the public Ministry; the contumely, the unbelief, the reproach, the rejection, the treachery. He had watched the awful tempest slowly gathering around the holy, human soul of the Man of sorrows. He had accompanied Him in that last journey to Jerusalem, the cloud deepening as the hour and power of darkness approached. He was the honoured,

privileged witness of the untold anguish in
the Garden: have we not reason to surmise
also that of the Cross? How fresh, therefore,
his every memory must have been as he
penned or dictated to-day's words! Yet,
after all, how little *did* he comprehend. He
only saw the surface-waves,—the unsounded
deeps he knew nothing of. Who ever could?
Who ever can? There were elements there
that can be gauged by no human sounding-
line. The words Messiah speaks by the prophet
may be taken in another than their true
meaning—" I have trodden the winepress
alone." But, amplifying what you said in a
few broken words last night, is it not just this
peerless, superhuman experience of sorrow and
anguish which gives the Great Sufferer a capa-
city to enter into *all* minor sufferings? These
mighty heart-throbs pulsate through every part
of the mystical body. The very magnitude
and unspeakableness of His own pangs render
Him the more sensitive to those of His people!

Yes, I cease to be surprised at your clinging so to your *great* verse, and especially to this, its central theme of mysterious adoring wonder, " partaker of Christ's *sufferings ;*"—that you have been reconciled and strengthened to bear and endure, in a way you never otherwise could, from the thought that the Captain of your salvation was Himself made perfect *through these.* Your feeling has been expressed over and over by His afflicted children. ' What are our severest pangs, intense as they may be, compared to what He, the sinless, spotless Lamb of God, voluntarily endured for us ? They are but dust in the balance. Speak of *my* weary nights, and then think of *Him* and His ! '

What pledges, too, these speechless agonies were of His love for His suffering people ! tending, at all events, to soothe and alleviate their acutest bodily anguish. I daresay you remember the touching lines I read the other evening from the leaflet which ——— sent you ? A suffering child of God alone could have written them:—

> " 'Tis Thy dear hand, O Saviour,
>   That presseth sore ;
> The hand that bears the nail-prints
>   For evermore.
>
> And now beneath His shadow,
>   Hidden by Thee,
> The pressure only tells me
>   Thou lovest me ! "

But I can write no further at present. There is much more you will be able to recall and meditate upon. May the entire subject be like a Gethsemane angel sent to strengthen you, carrying to you this anodyne in your hour of need—

" Beloved, think it not strange concerning the fiery trial which is to try you, as though some strange thing happened unto you : but rejoice, inasmuch as ye are partakers of Christ's sufferings."

GLORY.

The Glory that is to Follow.   Full of Glory.

My Dear ——

What can be better than to complete
the verse of yesterday, " the sufferings of
Christ, *and the glory that should follow* " (1 Pet.
i. 11)?   I am sure you would like this ; but
I think you would like still more, or at all
events in conjunction with it, the words almost
immediately preceding.   You seemed as if you
would never tire hearing them read to you.
" *Whom having not seen, ye love ; in whom,
though now ye see Him not, yet believing, ye
rejoice with joy unspeakable and full of glory* "
(1 Pet. i. 8).   Was it not your remembrance,
which I had forgotten, of ——'s death-bed
hymn you quoted to me——

> " My Saviour whom absent I love,
> Whom not having seen I adore "——

that helped to endear the verse ?   Be it so,

but it requires no such associations to bring
out or enhance its beauty.   It always seems
to me, not like a piece of inspired prose at all,
but rather (exceptional in St. Peter's writings)
like a fragment of sacred song.   No words, at
all events, are better calculated to disarm trial
and suffering.   It is the anticipated sight of the
unseen Saviour.   Christ, I know well, is very
near you, and very precious.   You can, thanks
be to God, with lowly confidence repeat the
kindred words : " I know whom I have believed, and am persuaded that He is able to
keep that which I have committed unto Him."
How many would give all they have for the
calm, unshaken trust you enjoy !   For I feel
assured you would as soon believe that there
is no sun in the heavens, as that there is no
Saviour who died for you; no Saviour who now
lives for you ; no, Saviour who is soon to welcome you, and receive you.   Still, " we walk
by faith, not by sight."   What a day that
will be when faith will be merged in perfect
vision ; when not only " we shall be like Him,

but we shall *see* Him as He is!" You truly
said, not long ago, when your mind seemed
fully possessed with this 'blessed hope,' that
it was almost too wonderful and glorious the
thought of being ushered in a moment into
the presence of the King. It was something
higher and better than the mere exhaustion of
suffering which led you to repeat with such
intensity of longing, "Oh that I had wings
like a dove, for then would I flee away, and
be at rest!" Surely no words can further so
accurately and beautifully express your feelings—waiting like this imprisoned bird for the
opening of the cage, than just the concluding
ones of our verse: "*Yet believing, ye rejoice
with joy unspeakable and full of glory.*" The
unspeakable bliss of Heaven! Human tongue
and speech fail to describe it. When we come
to see it, it will be, it *must* be, as you surmised, with some new organs of spiritual vision.
It reminds one of the "unspeakable words"
which Paul heard, but which he pronounces
impossible for a man to utter. He felt there

was a poverty of meaning in all earthly language to express the reality.

And then, "*full of glory;*" floods of glory. The poor eye of earth could not bear the blinding blaze. But the glorified, transfigured spirit shall. And, what you specially dwelt on, the glory of that glory is to see the now Unseen; not in fitful passing glimpses—not the contemplation of faith which is so dependent on arbitrary mental conditions—but "for ever *with the Lord.*" "In Thy *presence* there is fulness of joy." You can recall, as very appropriate, good old Rutherford's last sayings in their verse-form, which it will gratify —— to know you so much like—

> " The sands of time are sinking;
> The dawn of heaven breaks;
> The summer morn I've sighed for,
> The fair, sweet morn awakes.
> Dark, dark hath been the midnight,
>   But dayspring is at hand,
> And Glory, Glory dwelleth
>   In Immanuel's land !"

With the prospect of such a Day-break, the gleam of that bright and Morning Star, the bliss of that "summer morn;" above all, the vision of the King in His beauty—

" Beloved, think it not strange concerning the fiery trial which is to try you, as though some strange thing happened unto you : but rejoice, inasmuch as ye are partakers of Christ's sufferings ; that, when His glory shall be revealed, ye may be glad also with exceeding joy."

The chief Corner-Stone laid in Zion.

MY DEAR ——

I return to-day to that glorious Foundation of which you spoke so specially in connection with the upbuilding of your great spiritual Temple. The figurative words surely seem peculiarly suitable in the lips of Peter, " the Rock-man :" " *Behold, I lay in Zion a chief corner-stone, elect, precious ; and he that believeth on Him shall not be confounded* " (1 Pet. ii. 6).

I know you are fully prepared, neither to be discouraged nor surprised should severe bodily pain at times lead to doubts and fears and misgivings : as you expressed it, Satan trying to avail himself of human weakness in his assaults. How blessed, in these extremities, to look to the Corner-Stone, the *sure* Foundation ; to know that our everlasting security and safety are not dependent on our poor selves, our shifting frames and feelings, but rest on an immutable Saviour! He is faithful who here promises that "*whosoever believeth on Him shall not be confounded.*" "He is *the* Rock: His work is perfect" (Deut. xxxii. 4).

We have more than once talked of Peter's own personal reflections and experience as he wrote these letters. Undoubtedly he knew too well what human frailty and instability were, not to think with tender sensitiveness on those who were bending before the hurricane; "of little faith;" "beginning to fear," "sinking in the waves." He would assuredly have perished in the unstable element had his safety depended on his own resources. But there was a strong Hand at his side. That Hand was stretched out. (We recalled old ——'s "grip of Christ's Hand.") He was safe in the vessel—"the wind ceased."

How unspeakable your comfort, amid your present wild tempests of suffering, that you have never yet, even when they were severest, lost consciousness of having a Rock at hand. Blessed indeed the thought! On Christ, and in

Christ (the Clefts of the Rock) all is safe for
time and for eternity.   As some one you spoke
of said, " Christ never yet betrayed a soul that
rested upon Him." These waves of fear and
disquietude, it may even be of unbelief, may
momentarily blind you with their spray ; but
they cannot touch the immovable hiding-place.
I can understand your liking for the grand old
hymn, sung to you last evening among others—

> " Jesu, Lover of my soul,
> Let me to Thy shelter fly ;
> While the billows o'er me roll,
> While the tempest still is high ! "
> &c. &c.

To change to your favourite figure, other
stones of life's fair temple may be shattered, or
crumble to decay; not so the Stone laid in Zion.
You *have* made proof of His inviolable faithfulness in the past.   And despite of the
" strange things " that are happening to you,
He is standing now, as ever He did, or ever
He was, with the undiminished, hoarded love
of Eternity in His heart. In reading Philip

Henry's Memoirs, I was struck with the observation he makes on the death of his saintly friend Lady Puleston who died in 1658. " She was," says he, " the best friend I had on earth; but my Friend in heaven is still where He was, and He will never leave me nor forsake me."

Your testimony has been, and doubtless will be the same. Trust Him still. Trust Him implicitly. Trust Him in the dark. Trust Him now. Trust Him to the end.

—— tells me she read to you some days ago, the verses entitled "*When to trust Jesus,*" and that you greatly liked them. Let me write down just two of these as very appropriate to what we are now speaking of, as well as to your increased suffering :—

> "Oh trust thyself to Jesus
> When thou art tried with pain,
> No power for prayer—the only thought,
> How to endure the strain.
> Then is the hour for resting
> In His perfect love to thee ;
> Then is the time for singing,
> ' He thinks—He prays for me !'

D

Oh trust thyself to Jesus
In days of feebleness,
When thou canst only dumbly feel
Thy utter helplessness.
Then is the hour for proving
His mighty power in thee;
Then is the time for singing,
' His grace sufficeth me.' "

With this confidence that you have in Him,
you can raise your aching head from its pillow,
and say for the strengthening and encouragement of all fellow-sufferers—

" *Beloved, think it not strange concerning the
fiery trial which is to try you, as though some
strange thing happened unto you: but rejoice,
inasmuch as ye are partakers of Christ's sufferings; that, when His glory shall be revealed, ye
may be glad also with exceeding joy.*"

Christ the Suffering Example.

MY DEAR ——

"For even hereunto were ye called," so begins St. Peter's utterance next in order to-day.

Called for what? Just what God has so unexpectedly summoned *you* to now—a call to *suffering.* "CALLED," "appointed;" as if it were one of His greatest, divinest ends and purposes in the training of His children: "That no man should be moved by these afflictions; for yourselves know that we are *appointed* thereunto" (1 Thess. iii. 3). "Whom the Lord loveth" (we would expect the verse to end "He exempts from trial,— He gives immunity from pain"). No; the reverse, "Whom He loveth, He chasteneth." As the suffering child is the most fondly loved and watched one of the family, so in the household of God. I think it is Lady Powerscourt, in one of her beautiful letters, who remarks that God never speaks to His people so tenderly as when He summons them, or, in St. Peter's phrase, "calls" them, to the experience and endurance of affliction. It was a twice tenderly repeated 'call,' "Abraham, Abraham," when He bade the Father of the faithful ascend the mount of trial. It is so still. "He calleth His own sheep *by name*, and leadeth them out." 'Calleth' and leadeth where? To sunny pastures and placid waters? No. Often to lowering mountain-sides, amid the hurricane and the storm, to a dry and thirsty land, where no water is. Sometimes arresting— "calling out"—to sickness and seclusion in the midst of health and usefulness; sometimes leading up, and that too occasionally by a toilsome ascent of suffering, to the Pisgah-mount of Death (Deut. xxxii. 50).

But oh, how suffering, how all suffering, how *your* sufferings are transfigured, yea glorified, in the further words of Peter, "*Christ also suffered for us, leaving us an example that ye should follow His steps.*" Called to the meek and patient endurance of your present acutest pains from the contemplation *of Christ as the Great Example.* I know how wondrously, by means of your cherished verse, this has helped, 'braced' you, and proved an incentive in the past. The more devoutly you realise these sufferings, the less 'strange' must the fieriest of your fiery trials seem to be. You have expressed what I speak of again and again in various ways—shall I *paraphrase* it for you here? If *He* suffered and murmured not, whose anguish transcended that of all finite natures, how can I falter at the cup a loving Father puts in my hand? I will hear Him saying to me as He said to Peter, and as He says to every faithful disciple in the school of affliction, when perhaps the misgiving thought is in the heart, or the repining word on the tongue: "What is that to thee? Follow thou Me" (John xxi. 22).

One verse, however, in your daily-sung hymn and prayer, seems to express all you feel in better and terser words, with your eye upon HIM, the King of Sorrow and of Suffering—

"Though dark my path and sad my lot,
Let me be still and murmur not,
And breathe the prayer *divinely taught*,
Thy will be done!"

Christ was in all respects an Example in tribulation. Among other ways, have you not beautifully felt Him to be so in what you called His 'Suffering Prayers'? "Sit ye here," were His words in the depths of His agony, "while I go and pray yonder." "Being in an agony, He prayed the more earnestly." "Who in the days of His flesh, when He had offered up prayers and supplications, with strong crying and tears, unto Him that was able to save Him from death, and was heard in that He feared." I cannot help thinking of you in connection with all this, after what you told me and asked me to do yesterday.

Yes, I faithfully delivered your message to ——, that when, through severe pain, you lay awake at night unable to rest, you are much in prayer for him, and that you liked the idea of doing so when all others were asleep. Can you doubt,—can we doubt, these 'Suffering Prayers' are specially heard and answered? I repeat, does not an earthly father have his ear most open to the cry and call of a suffering child?

Perhaps, for anything you know, the very best answer that could be conveyed to this dear "brother and companion in tribulation" would just be the "more grace" contained in the words—(shall I call them 'the Angel's whisper,'—the message intrusted to some strengthening Angel of consolation?)—

"Beloved, think it not strange concerning the fiery trial which is to try you, as though some strange thing happened unto you: but rejoice, inasmuch as ye are partakers of Christ's sufferings."

[12th.

Suffering the Prelude to Glory.

MY DEAR ——

" *The sufferings of Christ, and the glory that should follow*" (1 Pet. i. 11). Taking, as we have been doing in succession, the three themes of our triplet, it is the *Glory* whose turn comes in order to-day.

Within the few brief words all the parts of that triplet are found united—" Christ," " Suffering," " Glory." St. Peter is speaking of " the Spirit of Christ " testifying, through the Old Testament prophets, of the Great Conflict and Victory. Don't you think, that of these prophetic utterances, he, most likely, had specially in his mind what a German writer so beautifully calls " The Golden Passional;" in which the suffering Messiah is represented as seeing " of the travail of His soul and being satisfied"? One likes to trace out the human

elements in all that appertains either to the
Person or work of the Elder Brother. *Our*
motives are often poor, low, selfish; even at
the best they are mingled and imperfect. We
may feel very sure, not so were those which
animated Him. Yet, just as we, ordinary mor-
tals, are braced to toil and effort, endurance
and suffering, by the hope of acquiring some
great or worthy object, so this most elevated
of incentives bore Him onwards in the superhuman conflict. He thought of the result of
His soul-travail, the Redemption of the multitude which no man can number. As it is
otherwise expressed, "Who for the joy which
was set before Him, endured the cross, despis-
ing the shame, and is now set down at the
right hand of the throne of God." Indeed you
specially recalled His own wondrous words, to
the same effect, in the Intercessory Prayer—
words which Peter may have listened to, linking the suffering with the glory:—" I have
glorified Thee on the earth, I have finished
the work which Thou gavest Me to do. And

now, O Father, glorify Thou Me with Thine own self, with the glory which I had with Thee before the world was."

Yes, you are full of gratitude, and you may well be, that you are able and strengthened to look, as your divine Master did, above and beyond the suffering, and to contemplate the wealth of joy and bliss, which through that soul-struggle of His has been purchased for you : glory rising upon glory, tier on tier of that Temple of Mercy, which has formed to you, all along, such a quickening heavenly vision. *Glory !* one moment of it will lead you to forget all present experiences of sadness. Are there not appointed singers in this Temple as in that of old ? It is an honour to be one of them. Some, as you know, consider "The Songs of Degrees" in the Psalter, to be those used by the Jewish pilgrims as step after step of the Temple on Zion was climbed. These steps of suffering which lead up to the better Entrance-gate have their songs too. Here is one which your Heavenly Father has put into your mouth, first for yourself and then for others who have, through you, been witnesses of " the faith and hope that are in God ; "—

" *Beloved, think it not strange concerning the fiery trial which is to try you, as though some strange thing happened unto you : but rejoice, inasmuch as ye are partakers of Christ's sufferings ; that, when His glory shall be revealed, ye may be glad also with exceeding joy.*"

Christ Precious to the Believer.

MY DEAR ——

We resume to-day our place at the source and fountain-head of all peace and joy. What did you pronounce to be the outcome and verdict of your whole life-experience, as well as of your present protracted discipline? These words express it: *"Unto you therefore which believe* HE *is precious"* (1 Pet. ii. 7).

Precious He has proved to you, independent of suffering. All you have gone through during these solemn weeks was not required to reveal the endearing qualities of the "Altogether Lovely." From your earliest years you have tested them, proved them, gloried in them. But as the storm endears the shelter to the traveller; as calamity, in its various forms, endears and enhances the value and bliss of human friendship; so with the Brother

born for adversity, the immovable Rock of
Ages. To you, through the ordeal of *suffering*,
His " preciousness " is deepened and intensified
—" The half had not been told me ! "

God, in arraying His spiritual children in
their garments of beauty, and putting, if I may
so express it, ' ornaments about their neck '
(including among these the golden chain of
tribulation), brings into special and conspicu-
ous prominence " the Pearl of great price." Our
hymn of yesterday seems never to weary you
(to which of us indeed can it ever grow
stale ?)—

" How sweet the name of Jesus sounds ! "

It has been rightly named ' a rich casket.'
How it enshrines this *preciousness of Jesus !*
Every line of it—almost every word of it—is
full of the mighty power of that Name which
is above every name : ' soothing sorrows,'
' healing wounds,' ' dispelling fears,' ' binding
broken hearts,' ' calming troubled spirits,' 'Bread
to the hungry,' ' Rest to the weary,' ' Rock,
Shield, Hiding-place,' the soul's ' Refuge ' in

life and its ' Music in death'! What a happy
assurance, *He is all that to you !*—that you
can, without a hesitation or misgiving, subscribe
the Apostle's words: " This is the confidence
that we have in Him!" I liked to hear the
first welcome with which you greeted your
worthy nurse, when she was expressing sorrow
for your suffering state: " I trust I can say,
' Safe in the arms of Jesus'"; and to ——,
" I am upheld by the prayers of others, and,
better still, by the love of the Saviour."

" *Christ precious.*" Last night, in your pangs
of pain, it was doubtless this same " confidence"
which led you to ask —— specially to read to
you

> " Why those fears? Behold 'tis Jesus
> Holds the helm and guides the ship ! "

' *Christ precious*' ; always precious. Amid the
fitfulness of human friendships, the precarious-
ness of human hopes, the instability of human
props and refuges, " He abideth faithful, He
cannot deny Himself." Your " great verse"
was last night superseded by the one ——

tells me she gave you, and which she was pleased to hear had proved a silent comforter in your sleepless hours, repeating it often to yourself: "I will never leave thee nor forsake thee!" May He more and more reveal to you the preciousness of His presence and supporting grace. The old favourite words, so sweetly sung with the others, even now linger in my ear, and have haunted me ever since I witnessed your sad increase of suffering—

> "All my hope on Thee is stayed ;
> All my help from Thee I bring:
> Cover my defenceless head
> *With the shadow of Thy wing!*"

"*He is precious!*" As this has been your life-song, so, when it pleases Him to take you to Himself, will it "revive your soul in death:" and as you enter glory, it will be the first note in your everlasting song. With Him at your side, as you are now passing through these dark Valleys of suffering, and with the darkest Valley yet to tread, think of all that darkness as (in the figure of the hymn just quoted) only the shadow of His wings! And if your own voice be too feeble to sing the words, you can ask others to do so—

" Beloved, think it not strange concerning the fiery trial which is to try you, as though some strange thing happened unto you: but rejoice, inasmuch as ye are partakers of Christ's sufferings; that, when His glory shall be revealed, ye may be glad also with exceeding joy."

Sufferings for us on the Tree.

MY DEAR ——

It is "Suffering" that is in turn our meditation to-day. And what a wonderful view of suffering is this which the Apostle describes! *" Who His own self bare our sins in His own body on the tree, that we, being dead to sins, should live unto righteousness; by whose stripes ye are healed "* (1 Pet. ii. 24).

Yes, marvellous consecration, and, I may call it *exaltation* of our sufferings, however intense and severe they may be! I need not say, the theme is by no means new to you; for it is the recurrent one of these letters and of our frequent converse. But let us think of the subject again, in connection with the experiences, and more especially the closing experiences, of the Suffering Master: the mockings and buffetings, the cruel scourge, the thorny crown, the pangs

E

of the bitter cross; these forming only the outer exponents of an inner soul-anguish which His people, in the fiery trials sent to try them, thank God, can know nothing of:—the "exceeding sorrow" of Gethsemane; the awful soul-desertion, whatever that may be, which had its interpretation in the rending cry. If ever the word "strange" could be applied to a fiery trial, it was surely in regard to the Innocent and Spotless One—"*stricken, smitten of God, and afflicted !*"

Look at some of the characteristics here noted in the experience of the Great Sufferer. His sufferings were voluntary: "*His own Self bare.*" His sufferings were physical,—bodily: "He bare in His own *body.*" His sufferings were substitutionary : "He bare *our* sins." His sufferings were complete : "By whose stripes *ye were healed.*" Oh what an argument and incentive—you have told me over and over you feel it so—to submit to this your own baptism of fire, because He has done the same; because without a murmur or a falter He drank

His cup of anguish to the dregs. By an inversion of the mocking cry,—" He *saved* others : Himself (not, He could not, but) He *would not* save ! " " His agony and bloody sweat, His cross and passion," have taken whatever is bitter out of your cup, and left it only a cup of love.

Then, think of the object of all that soul-travail and its result. " His own Self *bare our sins.*" No lines in your hymn-book are more deeply marked than these,—none have you more frequently and fervently in other days joined in singing—

> " These raging winds, this surging sea,
> Have spent their deadly force on Me :
> They bare no breath of wrath to thee ! "

The penalty of sin is exhausted, the mighty debt is paid. He hath taken the handwriting that was against us out of the way, nailing it to His cross. On your present couch of pain,—or, as God seems to purpose it so, your bed of death,—you can forget all your own sufferings as you repeat the wondrous words, " He loved me, and *gave Himself for me.*" A privilege, surely indeed, in any feeble way, to drink of the cup which He drank of, and to be baptized with His baptism!

Was it following up these various thoughts you asked —— to play Handel's "*He was despised and rejected*"? What a touching, plaintive dirge to be sure it is, on suffering, self-sacrificing love! Music, at its highest and best, seems to have caught up the echo of your verse and sent it thrilling down the ages—

"*Beloved, think it not strange concerning the fiery trial which is to try you, as though some strange thing happened unto you: but rejoice, inasmuch as ye are partakers of Christ's sufferings.*"

Faith and Hope in the Risen and Glorified.

MY DEAR ——

Another precious glimpse of the glory that was the result of suffering presents itself to-day (1 Pet. i. 21).

The sufferings of the Great Redeemer, about which we last spoke together, terminated in death. When the full cup was exhausted, He said, " It is finished ; and He bowed His head, and gave up the ghost." What a thought for *you* to ponder! That He, the Blessed One, familiar with every form of tribulation and woe, Himself succumbed outwardly (and very really) to the last enemy! " My soul is exceeding sorrowful *even unto death!*" (Mat. xxvi. 38).

But God " *raised Him from the dead, and gave Him glory*" (1 Pet. i. 21). When Peter wrote these words, the most memorable day of his life and of the world's life must have been again vividly recalled. " The Lord is risen indeed !" was the glad saying which he shared that first Easter Sunday with the wondering disciples. Death, with his Divine Lord, had only a momentary triumph. " He could not be holden of it." He took away its sting, and cast it into the flames of His sacrifice. " He dieth no more, *death* hath no more dominion over Him." Nay, further, God hath " crowned Him with glory and honour." On His head, as Mediator, there are " many crowns."

And what is the great practical lesson the Apostle deduces from the God of peace having brought again from the dead our Lord Jesus, that Great Shepherd of the sheep ? It is comfort to the flock in their every valley of earthly tribulation:—" *That your faith and hope might be in God*" (ver. 21). The gloom of the darkest valley of all enshrouded *Him*. These very billows which may be about to encompass *you*, encompassed *Him*. But you can look forward in calm confidence " beyond the shadows," knowing that " He which raised up the Lord Jesus shall raise up us also by Jesus " (2 Cor. iv. 14), " O Death, where is thy sting ? O Grave, where is thy victory?" May you not well anew exclaim with glad voice, as you did the other night after this verse was repeated to you, " *Victory, victory !*" Yes, for as God not only raised Him up, but " *gave Him glory,*" so too will it be with you and with every member of the ransomed family. I don't wonder you cling so fondly and sacredly to that, as the sublimest of the many sublime sayings in the Intercessory Prayer,—one we have quoted so often : " Father, I will that they also whom Thou hast given Me be with Me where I am, that they may behold My glory." This is the gift surpassing in magnitude every other : " *The gift of God, which is eternal life* through Jesus Christ our Lord."

The death and resurrection of Christ, and the heavenly bliss purchased and procured by Him, solve indeed all the mysteries of a future world. With such hopes as these, " Glory, honour, immortality, *eternal life*," you may once more listen with joyful heart to the refrain of our Apostle.   Let it be conveyed through the words of one of your bright hymns—

> " Hark ! 'tis the voice of angels,
>   Borne in a song to me,
>   Over the fields of glory,
>   Over the jasper sea."—

" *Beloved, think it not strange concerning the fiery trial which is to try you, as though some strange thing happened unto you: but rejoice, inasmuch as ye are partakers of Christ's sufferings; that, when His glory shall be revealed, ye may be glad also with exceeding joy.*"

Mercy Obtained.

MY DEAR ──

We have again to touch the grand key-notes to-day, without which both the song of earth and the anthem of glory would be impossible. More than one beautiful and suggestive thought is to be gathered from the two verses which come here in order (1 Pet. ii. 9, 10).

There is, first, the designation of 'Honour'; what an old writer calls 'the patent of nobility'—"*royal priesthood*" (ii. 9). Believers become kings and priests unto God, by virtue of the atoning Sacrifice and Intercession of the Great High Priest. Then, there is the "marvellous light" (ii. 9) into which they have been ushered, out of the darkness of sin:—the Sun of righteousness arising upon them with healing in His beams.

Our conversation, however, took rather the direction of the third statement the passage contains: "*But now have obtained mercy*" (ii. 10). It is your old fond theme; the up-building of the vast and glorious Temple of Mercy founded on the Rock of Ages.

Mercy is a sinner's word. God "*loves*" the pure and spotless Angels; but the guilty and lost and perishing cling fondly to the more appropriate term:—"God, who is rich in *mercy*." "For this cause," says St. Paul, "I obtained (not love, but) *mercy*." It is mercy he prays for in behalf of his friend: "The Lord grant unto him that he may find *mercy* of the Lord in that day." "Looking for the *mercy* of our Lord Jesus Christ, unto eternal life" (Jude 21). How often have you sung, on bygone Sunday evenings—

> "Oh depth of *mercy*, can it be
> That Gate was left ajar for me!"

It is a fine thought you lately enlarged upon: each one of us contributing our separate stone to this great eternal "Mercy-Temple."

Who can picture or describe the glories of that day, when, " complete in Him," the topstone is brought forth with shouting, and the cry will be, " Mercy, mercy!" " Grace, grace!" unto it ?

Equally beautiful was the idea (I am not sure whether it was your own or another's, but I liked it coming from suffering lips), that all the cutting and preparation of these living stones for this Heavenly Sanctuary is done *now,* and will cease then: that it will be with the new, as with the old Jerusalem-Temple its type;—" The House when it was in building was built of stone made ready before it was brought thither. So that there was neither hammer nor axe nor any tool of iron heard in the house while it was in building " (1 Kings vi. 7). Yes, to pursue the simile, the assurance may well animate you to calm endurance, that all the present shaping and drilling, the squaring and polishing, effected by iron tools of earthly suffering are there absolutely unknown. Every stone has received its finishing-touch on earth, and is ready, without jar or friction or implement of any kind, to be set in its assigned place, and that for ever ! "A building of God, an house not made with hands, eternal in the heavens. Now He that HATH *wrought us* for the self-same thing (*lit.*, ' prepared us,' ' worked us up' as living stones) is God" (2 Cor. v. 7). .

Since writing the above, I have come, very accidentally, in the life of a distinguished dignitary of the English Church, on these appropriate words. He says, in writing to a friend :—" In the spiritual house which the Divine Architect is building, He requires stones of every size, small as well as great; the fresh unstained soul of childhood, and the soul that has been hewn, and chiselled, and beaten into shape by the cares, temptations, and struggles of life. We are each predestined to our place in the great spiritual building, while part of our happiness hereafter will doubtless consist in our seeing all has been ordered so as to qualify us for our eternal position."

And what a perfectly wonderful ascription will that 'new song' of this august sanctuary be! Nay, not *new* song; for it will indeed be nothing more than the *old* song of the pilgrimage; the song you only seem to be singing with intenser earnestness as the lengthening shadows are visibly gathering around you: " Oh give thanks unto the Lord, for He is good, for His MERCY endureth for ever."

If suffering be thus only the carving of the stones, or the refining of the gold, for the decoration of walls and rafters and ceiling of that Temple of the glorified; listen to the word of Him who is alike Master-Builder and Refiner; who has His own all-wise ends both in using His tools for the stones, and gathering His fuel for the furnace—

" *Beloved, think it not strange concerning the fiery trial which is to try you, as though some strange thing happened unto you: but rejoice !* "

and vicarious Sacrifice. I liked the remark you made some time ago, which you had either heard or read (I think you said it was in a sermon of ——) about the obedience of Jesus; that even *before* He suffered on the cross He exclaimed, " I HAVE *finished* the work which Thou gavest Me to do." It became Him, in our room and stead, to fulfil all righteousness. That perfect obedience being rendered, the mighty work was further and fully consummated by the pouring out of His life's-blood. Thus alike He paid the penalty due to sin, and wrought out a perfect, everlasting righteousness. I do not know if I have rightly caught up your idea or made it clear; but at all events your meaning is very clear in the old familiar couplet you ended with, as having now a significance doubly real and doubly precious to you—

" On Christ the solid Rock I stand,
   All other ground is sinking sand."

The " solid Rock," by the by, reminds me of what —— told me of a series of sermons

B

you heard last summer, on the texts of which
your main comment was, " I can't forget ' Lead
me to the Rock that is *higher than I.*' "   You
had no dream then of the " overwhelmed heart"
with which the Psalmist introduces the words.
But the prayer has been answered, and you
never felt more firmly set than you now are
on that Rock of Ages.

With such a sure foundation as this,—the
glorious consciousness that the Redemption is
complete, nothing to add, nothing to supplement,—let these murmuring waves of present
suffering, as they break on the Rock, only
show how secure thereon your footing is.
Suffering such as yours is, *must*, indeed, be
hard enough to bear ; yet how harder far but
for the assurance " safe in Christ."   And if,
under the divine teaching and discipline, it be
the means of endearing *Him*, then

" *Beloved, think it not strange concerning the
fiery trial which is to try you, as though some
strange thing happened unto you : but rejoice.*"

those of His people, as to render Him capable of feeling sensitively and " in all points " with them and for them.   He " suffered *in the flesh.*"

You have always felt it a comforting and strengthening exercise to recall some of His sayings when the gloom of Gethsemane and Calvary was gathering around Him.   " Father, if it be possible;" " Not as I will, but as Thou wilt;" " This cup which My Heavenly Father hath given Me, shall I not drink it ?" " Father, into Thy hands I commend My spirit."   On the silent repetition of each of these, let your prayer be to the same gracious Giver of the cup—His Father and your Father, His God and your God—' *Arm me also with the same mind :*—with His patience and meekness, His gentleness and submission, His filial, unswerving devotion.   May I be led to accept, as He did, every pang without a misgiving, assured that nothing can come wrong to me which is appointed by Him !'

> " I take this pain, Lord Jesus,
>   From Thine own hand ;
> The strength to bear it bravely
>   Thou wilt command.
> I take this pain, Lord Jesus ;
>   What Thou dost choose
> The soul that really loves Thee
>   Will not refuse ! "

Thus feeling, as I know you do, not only the wonderful strength and comfort, but the wonderful *privilege* contained in the central clause of St. Peter's great solace,—tell it out to others for their confidence in a similar hour—

" Beloved, think it not strange concerning the fiery trial which is to try you, as though some strange thing happened unto you: but rejoice, inasmuch as ye are partakers of Christ's sufferings."

The Revelation of Christ's Glory.

MY DEAR ——

. We have reached in its turn to-day, the last, the concluding clause in your " meteor verse." It forms the third link in our present triple chain of comfort and hope. But there is verily a whole Heaven contained in it. *" That when His glory shall be revealed, ye may be glad also with exceeding joy "* (1 Pet. iv. 13).

It is evidently a favourite expression of St. Peter's, for a few verses farther on, he speaks of himself as " also a partaker of the glory that shall be revealed " (2 Pet. vi.) What a burst of celestial radiance will that be! You were lately recalling the dying words of the dearest friend you and I ever had—*" glorious light."* The glory of that same glorious light is (it may be feebly—but very assuredly) breaking upon you. I know you have as little care as I have

for ecstatic deathbed scenes. They are given,
but given rarely. The frail, weak, tossed,
perishable body often dims the soul's window-
panes, and prevents seeing, as the eye of faith
would desire to do—" the King in His beauty,
and the land that is very far off!" Though,
therefore, as George Herbert has it—" Sweet
Phosphor *is* bringing the day," yet it would be
a mockery to speak of you now, in St. Peter's
words, as " glad also with exceeding joy."
That simply cannot be, with such clouds of
suffering hovering around your horizon. The
song of joy cannot be sung with trembling,
anguished lips. But " the morning is spread
upon the mountains!" It brings before me
the walk you sent me, night before last
through the pinewood, just as the sun was
setting. I shall never forget it. The tall
stems of the firs, low down in the valley, were
all in shadow. But their tops were gilded—I
should rather say ruddy—with the parting sun-
beams. I confess that forest of pines sent my
thoughts wandering to your sickbed. I thought

of the shadows—the deepening shadows, but only as imparting a contrasted glory! Blessed are those who, when the sun of life is fast going down and the mortal part is in gloom, have all that is highest, noblest, best, indestructible, reddened with the glow of the Unsetting Sun.

Take all the love and faithfulness of Jesus in the past, as a pledge that His glory will yet be *fully* revealed: when the song, now often sung in the plaintive minor, will attain its notes of "exceeding joy." That was a delightful whisper last night you confided in your weakness to ——, "Our light affliction, which is but for a moment, worketh for us a far more exceeding and eternal weight of glory" (2 Cor. iv. 17). With such a glory, partly in possession but its full radiance in reversion—

"Beloved, think it not strange concerning the fiery trial which is to try you, as though some strange thing happened unto you: but rejoice!"

Peace in Christ.

MY DEAR ——

No sufferer could desire a more gracious and comforting benediction than comes to you to-day. *"Peace be with you all that are in Christ Jesus"* (1 Pet. v. 14).

It is the very last sentence of the first Epistle. What beautiful closing life-words in the case too of "Epistles of Christ!" No wonder that the Christians of the first ages, with the image of recent death (often violent death) fresh upon them, should carve this very inscription on the slabs of the catacombs under the names of their sainted departed,—IN CHRISTO, IN PACE: calling, moreover, their burial-places ' *Cemeteries* ' (' Sleeping-places ').

You have often spoken of the Redeemer's "legacy of peace:"—"Peace I leave with you, My peace I give unto you," &c. Singularly, to be sure, do old, long-vanished recollections

of small things come back in such an hour as
this! I am pleased—I was going to say
touched—to hear that you so thankfully recal
the little incident, I had quite forgotten, of
some thirty-five years ago, in ———'s primitive
cottage school,—that this, on the occasion of
our visit, was the one verse which was repeated
all round, and that it impressed you. Strange,
that such a dim and tiny memory should come
floating with its message of comfort in the
hour you most need it! The worthy old
teacher, I must tell you, died in the full
faith of her text.

How many has that same verse comforted in
their similar closing days! Perhaps St. Peter
himself, in his unchronicled martyrdom, above
all other utterances 'remembered the words of the
Lord Jesus how He said'—"My peace I give
unto you, not as the world giveth, give I unto
you." At all events the honoured Apostle, in
concluding his present Epistle, echoes the
dying bequest of his Master. It is not impossible, that it was with this 'Great Valedic-

tory' in his recollection, he writes as in the verse of to-day—"*Peace be with you all that are in Christ Jesus*" (1 Pet. v. 14).

And this peace is *yours.*

Yes, peace—true spiritual peace in the midst of acute suffering. You have often remarked to me, if I may expand your own words—If bodily pain be hard enough to bear alone, what must it be when, superadded to that, is dispeace of the soul; the anguish of spiritual disquietude; the "fiery trial" without any spiritual compensations; 'the cloud without the bow;' the future *without hope!* Chastisement for the present very grievous—but no "afterward" yielding the peaceable fruits of righteousness!

"Peace in Christ Jesus." That is indeed a grand assurance to rest upon, living or dying. I never can forget, not only the saying, but the way you said it—"If you have Christ, then you have everything else." What a peace is this! Peace from the condemnation of the law, —peace from the accusations of conscience,— peace from the assaults of the great Tempter,

—peace in every varying condition of life:
—peace in sickness, in sorrow, in death: and
the perfect peace of Heaven in prospect. Yes,
the *perfect* peace.   For the Christian's spiritual
calm here, though perfect in one sense—perfect in *kind*, is not so in degree.   It is neces-
sarily, indeed, from outward and inward causes,
disturbed, intermittent: the calm of the lake-
surface you and I know so well, easily rippled
with the passing breeze.   But at last it will
be the peace of the crystal sea; "the rest
which remains for the people of God." ——
happily selected at prayers last night the passage: "Thou wilt keep him in perfect peace
(or as he rendered it, 'Peace Peace'), whose
mind is stayed on Thee."   So great and sore a
sufferer as you are, how can you wonder that
endurance threatens at times to give way, as you
are 'driven by the wind and tossed'?   Some one
has reminded us, "that the breakers ahead are
always near the haven."   But I like another
figure.   You remember it in the old lake-side.
The storm only moors the oak-roots more

securely to the rifted rock. So with the 'life hid with Christ in God:' and so I believe has it been and will be with you. You said the other day with deep thankfulness, " I have had great enjoyment in life." But neither have you been without your share of its disappointments and cross currents and buffeting waves, —rough discipline. " Waves and clouds and storms," however, as your hymn has often told you, are the elements through which God " steers " His people. " He maketh the clouds His chariot, He walketh on the wings of the wind." It made —— sad, yet glad, to hear you saying, " I am going through great suffering; but God's grace enables me to bear it." Yes, that grace *will* upbear and *will* sustain you. And now within sight of the peaceful harbour, looking back on " sanctified afflictions," can you not bequeath *your* dying legacy also—

" *Beloved, think it not strange concerning the fiery trial which is to try you, as though some strange thing happened unto you.*"

Rejoicing in the Fiery Trial.

MY DEAR ———

It would never do—often as it has been repeated, to pass by when its turn comes in the Epistle, your specially prized verse "*concerning the fiery trial*" (1 Pet. iv. 12, 13).

Say as we may, however, despite of the Apostle's exhortation, such a trial as you have now been called to endure, *does* seem "strange." In the midst of health and strength, and active work for God and man— to be deflected without a note of warning from one of the quiet, peaceful valleys of life, carpeted with flowers and bathed in sunshine, and summoned to a land of drought and of the shadow of death! Yes, truly, it not only seems, but it *is* mysterious and startling. Well can I imagine the reality of all you described: the struggle beyond words, when the solemn verity first dawned upon you, that your work here was done for ever! Not only so, but the sad sequel of the weeks which followed (happily still less anticipated)—the pain, the sleeplessness, these aggravated by the sultry oppression day and night. Saddest of all, the bitter thoughts of earthly parting,— "fiery trial" indeed!

Thank God you have, nevertheless, been led up, step by step, to calm endurance,—meek resignation. And if you can, so far at least as is compatible with so great a fight of afflictions, even enter into Peter's 'rejoicing:' what has mainly led you, and strengthened you to sing this tremulous song in your deepest night? The night is dark as ever— the furnace is hot as ever,—but you have been enabled (with, I think I may call it an habitual adoring wonder) to "rejoice, *inasmuch as ye are partakers of Christ's sufferings!*" Not a pang have you borne, but He has borne before you; not a tear have you wept, but He has wept before you; not a shadow has encom-

passed you, but fell on His lone night of
agony; not a flame of your furnace but
wrapped His guiltless head! Your sufferings,
moreover, have been full, to use your own
repeated phrase, of "merciful alleviations:"
—tender hands to smooth the ruffled pillow,
and cool the throbbing brow; gentle voices to
whisper balm-words of comfort. You spoke
affectionately to ——, she tells me, yesterday, of the kindness and the sympathy that
had been shown to you by others, adding,
"*that* our Saviour was denied." Yes, truly,
"Waters of a full cup" were wrung out to
Him! In that, indeed, and in manifold other
ways, a full participation in His sufferings is
therefore impossible. Our worst is but the
rim of the thundercloud, compared to the
hour of great darkness which shrouded and
descended on Him. "*All* Thy waves and
Thy billows are gone over Me!" "I am a
worm and no man, a reproach of men and
despised of the people" (Ps. xxii. 6). "Is it
nothing to you, all ye that pass by? behold

and see if there be any sorrow like unto my sorrow?" (Lam. i. 12.) When in the extremity of His anguish in the Garden He came to His disciples,—those who ought to have kept most sacred vigil for Him,—"He findeth them asleep!" "I looked for some to take *pity*" (the poorest thing one can receive), "but there was none; and for comforters, but I found none!" (Ps. lxix. 20.) *Your* sufferings, as you have again and again said, are "deserved, and more than deserved;" *His*, the anguish of "the *Holy One* of God." If at any time, under the pressure of severe bodily pain, you are tempted to "faint when you are rebuked of Him," keep steadfastly before you the Vision and the Voice of the Master, as He says, "All this have I borne for *thee*; wilt thou not be willing, yea joyful, to bear and endure for *Me?*" What a priceless legacy (through His own self-sacrifice and divine submission) has He thus bequeathed to the whole pain-stricken, woe-worn family of God!

Meanwhile, considering " Him that endured such contradiction of sinners against Himself, lest ye be weary and faint in your mind," listen yet again to the tones of this silver trumpet, sounded by one of God's cross-bearing yet triumphant champions—

" Beloved, think it not strange concerning the fiery trial which is to try you, as though some strange thing happened unto you : but rejoice, inasmuch as ye are partakers of Christ's sufferings."

Glory with exceeding Joy.

MY DEAR ——

 I last wrote, and we last spoke together, on the verse which never seems to pall upon you.

 It was, however, only the first, and what may be called earthly phase of it—the cheering light it sheds in passing through your present valley of tribulation, as a partaker of Christ's sufferings. Though the concluding clause has already, and very lately too, been both written and meditated upon, you will not object to the repetition. It seems impossible to pass it by now; and indeed it cannot well be severed from what precedes. The two thoughts, thus united, render the passage to you and such as you, absolutely perfect and complete as a leaflet of comfort. It is a 'look beyond the cloud,' a glimpse of tho Delectable Mountains from the land Beulah :—" *That, when His glory shall be revealed, ye may be glad also with exceeding joy* " (1 Pet. iv. 13).

In the former part, it was the solacing privilege of being, in some lowly form, partaker of your suffering Master's cross and passion;—now, it is identity and participation with Him in His crown of glory. Neither you nor I have ever ventured to speculate on the various theories of pre-millennial or post-millennial Advent-bliss. Rather, I know your thoughts have a truer, better, brighter reality to rest upon—the revelation of the Saviour's glory at the moment of death :—" To depart and to be with Christ, which is far better." That was an elevating and soothing talk you began, but for which your strength again was unequal, about the morning scene at the Lake of Tiberias. Yes, how it may well reconcile to all the tossings and darkness of life's midnight hour, the thought of HIM standing at daybreak on the heavenly, as He once did on that earthly shore, with the eternal banquet of love *ready prepared;* Peter's old, half-trembling avowal now the unqualified and unhesitating avowal and joy of eternity—" Lord, Thou knowest all things, Thou knowest that I love Thee!" I cease to wonder at your earnest, vehement cry—whose tones have followed me in thought ever since I left you: " Come, Lord Jesus! oh, *do come* quickly!"

What a vision and " revealing" will that be, when the prayer (not your prayer, but that of the Divine Intercessor which we have often spoken of before) is heard and answered—"That they may behold My glory!" not the passing glimpse, but, with better than Hadyn's sweet cadences to it, the fulfilled aspiration—

> " Let me be with *Thee* where Thou art,
> My Saviour, my eternal rest!
> Then only will this longing heart
> Be fully and for ever blest!"

I know the unwavering confidence you have, which few venture to entertain so fully, of meeting your ' loved and lost'—now the loved and glorified. Not many days ago, you asked

G

me touchingly, 'Do you think they will be
found in groups?' I forgot to remark that
the only time I ever met the venerable poet,
James Montgomery, he dwelt upon this very
idea as a beautiful possibility:—the old tastes
and occupations and partialities of earth ('idio-
syncrasies,' I fancy, is the proper word), as
being then and there restored; leading the
ransomed flock to cluster together on separate
pastures, and around separate "living fountains
of waters." But even should this be realised
as the devout imagination pictures or desires,
it is "*the Lamb*" who leads them there and
feeds them there (Rev. vii. 17). Heaven is *the
revelation of* His *glory.* The—

> " For ever with the Lord :
> Amen, so let it be !"

of the good poet's own matchless hymn, as it
expresses the longing of the Church on earth,
so does it express the essence of the completed
bliss and enjoyment of the glorified. Without
that "excellent glory" it would be the blotting
out of the sun from the heavenly firmament.

" With *Thee* is the fountain of life." Your own favourite Temple is displaced and superseded by a nobler one:—" And I saw no Temple therein; for the Lord God Almighty and the Lamb are the Temple of it" (Rev. xxi. 22).

With such a ' revelation ' in prospect—such a dawn now streaking your eastern sky—the harbinger of " perfect day "—

" *Beloved, think it not strange concerning the fiery trial which is to try you, as though some strange thing happened unto you: but rejoice, inasmuch as ye are partakers of Christ's sufferings; that, when His glory shall be revealed, ye may be glad also with exceeding joy."*

The Righteousness of Christ.

MY DEAR ———

We have found the former Epistle of St. Peter so rich in doctrine, promise, and consolation, that this is the first day I have trenched on our otherwise now familiar ground in the second. But the opening verse is, as you told me, to your heart's desire. All through your illness you have continued lovingly and unfalteringly to cling to that glorious truth (as the verse is much better rendered in the Revised Version)—"*the righteousness of our God and Saviour Jesus Christ*" (2 Pet. i. 1). How often not only have you recurred to it, but as a suffering and (you do not now dread the word) dying man, how often have you bewailed the modern defection from a doctrine ever looked to as the very day-star of your spiritual horizon; a grand

Gospel prop and support which you could not live without, and which you dare not die without. I might well gratefully recall to your memory, how, a quarter of a century ago, you directed my own mind, with fervid lip and enthusiasm, to this very truth. It is comforting and strengthening to see, how, despite the advanced thinking of others, there has been no receding here with you. When, removed from earth, you can no longer with the old emphatic earnestness enlarge upon it, I shall love to tell all near and dear to you how every other truth seemed still to dim and pale before this wondrous one :—

> " Jesus, Thy blood and righteousness,
> My beauty are, my glorious dress ;
> Mid flaming worlds in these arrayed,
> With joy shall I lift up my head."

I have not forgotten, what indeed I noted in a former letter, the observation you had heard or culled elsewhere, that Christ wrought out a righteousness for us *in His life :* that having by His perfect life-obedience weaved a spotless robe for His people, "He took that robe, and, so to speak, dipped it in His blood." Having done so, He could then exclaim over the completed work alike of *doing* and *dying* —"It is finished!" This must surely be a favourite, cherished, constant thought of yours. —— tells me that when she was reading, the other night, one of the last verses of the same hymn of Wesley's—

"Even then shall this be all my plea,
That Jesus lived and died for me"—

you broke in with the same remark—"Yes, *lived* as well as died—wrought out a righteousness for us in His life."

Amid bodily suffering and wearisome nights; still more, amid the consciousness of frailty and infirmity—the memories of unworthiness and sin, what perfect peace and reliance is there here! Soon, in the garment of the Elder Brother, to "stand without fault before the throne!" "They shall walk with Me in white, for they are worthy" (through My worthiness). And seeing that tribulation

—" great tribulation "—is represented as God's own appointed means of leading to the washing of the saints' robes and making them thus white in the blood of the Lamb (Rev. vii. 14), let your own blessed and happy experience of the soul-elevating theme speak, in the words of this verse, "*to them that have obtained like precious faith with us, through the righteousness of our God and Saviour Jesus Christ*"—

"*Beloved, think it not strange concerning the fiery trial which is to try you, as though some strange thing happened unto you : but rejoice, inasmuch as ye are partakers of Christ's sufferings ; that, when His glory shall be revealed, ye may be glad also with exceeding joy.*"

The Divine Trustful Sufferer.

MY DEAR ——

We noted before, in the closing chapter of the first Epistle, how Peter there speaks of himself as "a witness of the sufferings of Christ" (v. i), and how well warranted he was to do so, as one of the privileged three in Gethsemane, who were withdrawn but a stone's cast from the supreme anguish. We had reason, moreover, further to conjecture, that despite his own lamentable cowardice and fall, he had been spectator of much at least of the dread sequel. What a contrast he must always have felt—ever surely a sad and humbling memory—between his own violent, perjured protestations, and the meek bearing of Him who "as a sheep before his shearers was dumb;" who, in the words of our recent conversation, which come in turn to-day, "*Did*

*no sin, neither was guile found in His mouth :
Who, when He was reviled, reviled not again ;
when He suffered, He threatened not ; but committed Himself to Him that judgeth righteously"*
(1 Pet. ii. 22, 23).

Oh, what an argument, beyond all other
arguments, is here, for patience in tribulation !
We have adduced the lesson again and again,
but it is the one a believing sufferer never
tires of. St. Peter's reiteration of the subject
in these Epistles (which compels our dwelling
upon it) is remarkable. It is evidently a chief
topic alluded to in his introductory verse—
"Wherefore I will not be negligent *to put you
always in remembrance* of these things" (2 Pet.
i. 12).

What, then, is this constantly-recurrent
theme ? HE *submitted without a complaint or
a murmur !*

This is not nature's way. The reflection and
pleading of the smitten one rather is—"Lord,
if Thou hadst been here !" " Wherefore con-
tendest Thou with me ?" "Hath the Lord for-

gotten to be gracious ?" " All these things are
against me." " Where is now my God ?" But
with unquestioning resignation *He* endured !
He had the one desire—the one animating,
dominating thought and aspiration, " Father,
glorify Thy name."

Seeking to follow in His steps, though you
may feel it is at best, as with Peter, " afar off,"
I know your present prayer and steadfast
resolve is to submit to the divine will;—to submit without daring for a moment to impeach
the wisdom and faithfulness of a Father-God:
feeling that all *must* be well just *because* HE
wishes it.   Truly, not " well " in accordance
with our poor fallible judgments; not " well "
this arrest in the midst of health and vigour;
not " well " this life-work unfinished; not
" well " this prolonged, increasing discipline
of pain; not "well" these tears of mourners—
the pang of final earthly separation ! No. But
" it *is* well ;" for in the words of Hezekiah, "*He*
hath both spoken unto me and Himself hath
done it " (Isa. xxxviii. 15).   He who " doth

not afflict willingly," He who as much appoints every sorrow as He marks out the pathway of that comet in the realms of space—has mixed the cup, and led you (if I dare so with reverence express it) to your Gethsemane of suffering.

Endeavour more and more to put yourself in the Master's place, and to imbibe the Master's spirit; to commit yourself, as you have done, to " *Him that judgeth righteously.*" You remember the image we have not only frequently spoken of together, but frequently seen together in long years gone by, when skirting the abrupt shore of a Highland loch; the *visible* " great mountains," the *invisible* " great deeps" of that sublime Psalm (Ps. xxxvi.) The "judgments" of God are the one: the " righteousness" of God the other. In vain we try to fathom the judgments. They are lost from sight in the unsounded depths.. But the divine " righteousness" cannot be gainsaid. We own it—we believe it—we trust it—we *see* it, at least by the eye of faith. Let us leave the vain attempt to comprehend what is mysterious; and rest meanwhile content with the assurance, " The Lord is righteous in all His ways, and holy in all His works."

" O *Righteous* Father!" was the closing exclamation with which Jesus braced and prepared Himself for His own mysterious night of agony (John xvii. 25): a blessed pattern-invocation, surely, bequeathed by Him to all His true people for their hour of affliction and death!

Anew identifying yourself with the Saviour in His pain, His endurance, His 'glorifying God in the day of visitation,'—lay your weary head on this best of pillows—

" *Beloved, think it not strange concerning the fiery trial which is to try you, as though some strange thing happened unto you: but rejoice, inasmuch as ye are partakers of Christ's sufferings.*"

The Chief Shepherd and the Crown of Glory.

My Dear ——

We have to renew our talk to-day in its due order, on St. Peter's reference to the "*Crown of Glory*," and its bestowment by the hands of "*the Chief Shepherd*" (1 Pet. v. 4).

The shepherd-symbol must have been one often present to his mind ever since the charge on the shores of Gennesaret, "Feed My lambs —feed My sheep:" that never-to-be-forgotten day when he himself—a wandering sheep— was reponed once and for ever in the Chief Pastor's love! We need not be fastidious about the mixture of metaphor, the kingly *crown* bestowed by the *Good Shepherd* who gave His own life for the sheep. As applied to God, I do not wonder at your preference for the New Testament paternal· symbol; that assuredly is the most precious and comforting of all. But the Old Testament shepherd name and emblem has much in it, too, that is gracious and consolatory, specially in the hour of suffering and death.   Since laid on your sick-bed, how often have you recalled to yourself, or had read to you by others, that matchless twenty-third Psalm! It seems ever fresh, ever new; as fresh as when we were first taught it together in days gone by, amid scenery akin to that which it describes.   How it brings back far other life-memories too, better than literal green pastures or still waters !   And now that severe affliction has overtaken you : when these sunny meadows are left behind, the dreary mists falling, and the clouds obscuring the mountain-tops ; has not the experience imaged in the Psalm come all true :—"He restoreth my soul; He leadeth me in the paths of righteousness for His name's sake " ?   As I fear is only too certain, should the green spots recede and the dark valley open, the Great and Good Shepherd is there with the rod and staff of His supporting promises :—" Grand promises to rest upon," as you said, regarding a cluster of others, to ——— yesterday. The same Psalm assures you of your watched, tended, provided-for future, whatever that may be. You are led by the hands of your two favourite—guardian-angels, shall I call them?—GOODNESS and MERCY;—the vista unfolding yet farther beyond, with its triumphant assurance—"I will dwell in the house of the Lord for ever!" It is worthy of note, that Peter's double metaphor is not absent from David's older Psalm. The "table prepared," and "the head anointed with oil," seem to speak of kingly honours, as well as pastoral guidance. The gift of the Good Shepherd, the true "Shepherd-King," is "*a crown of glory that fadeth not away.*"

——— tells me you asked her to read the verse twice over to you about "the Vale of Shadows."

["Lead me through the Vale of Shadows,
   Bear me o'er life's fitful sea,
  Then the Gate of Life Eternal,
   May I enter, Lord, with Thee,
    Close to Thee, close to Thee,
   May I enter, Lord, with Thee!"]

I have just spoken of the Psalmist's 'table prepared.' Let me here say, it was an unspeakable gratification our late quiet partaking, all together, of the Holy Sacrament. Surely Christ's own promise was never more truly fulfilled—"Where two or three are gathered together in My name, there am I in the midst of them" (Matt. xviii. 20). Your remark which broke the silence of the close, had, I am sure, a response from each of us—"This will be remembered through all eternity." I felt to be peculiarly touching the appropriateness of the verse read—"I will not drink henceforth of this fruit of the vine, until that day when I drink it new with you in My Father's kingdom!" (Matt. xxvi. 29). Did not the rite, too—the memorial of "His Cross and Passion," bring the words of your 'great verse' peculiarly home—"partakers of Christ's sufferings"? So —— remained after we left, and sang to you Dr. Bonar's Communion Hymn:

" Feast after feast thus comes and passes by,
  Yet passing, points to the glad feast above,
  Giving sweet foretastes of the festal joy,
  The Lamb's great bridal feast of bliss and love."

Your own picture of " The Last Communion "
was vividly before me all the time; with the
locking of the church door,—the return home,
—the wintry landscape,—the snow sprinkling
the graves,—the fast-vanishing sun! Well,—
" *Till He come !* " And then,—the never-to-be-
withdrawn Table; the Great Master's immediate presence; the uninterrupted fellowship and
communion in the long for-ever of Heaven!—

" *Beloved, think it not strange concerning the
fiery trial which is to try you, as though some
strange thing happened unto you; but rejoice,
inasmuch as ye are partakers of Christ's sufferings; that, when His glory shall be revealed, ye
may be glad also with exceeding joy.*"

H

A God of Boundless Compassion.

MY DEAR ——

Another glimpse to-day of your favourite Temple of MERCY. What more soothing sight for a suffering couch, or for a dying pillow? What more consolatory theme for a weary, burdened body, above all, for a weary, burdened, it may be, at times, sin-stricken spirit, than the assurance that "HE *is long-suffering to usward, not willing that any should perish, but that all should come to repentance"* (2 Pet. iii. 9).

Never man lived who felt the truth of this more than he who wrote these words. To repeat a remark we have made more than once :—how righteously might the coward and renegade have had pronounced upon him the doom of Judas—been left to 'perish'—surrendered to his sins, and not suffered to "*come* to re-

pentance!" The 'look' of righteous reproach—
yet longsuffering love, which fell upon him in
the courtyard of Caiaphas, might have been the
last glimpse of scorned mercy and unrequited
kindness. But with heartfelt gratitude might
he write, as his own brief comment on that
story of the past, after thirty years had gone
by—" *longsuffering* TO USWARD."

You truly said, how hard, how utterly impossible it would be to meet God, but for this
most blessed confidence, that in His own essen-
tial Nature, and through the atonement of Jesus,
" He is gracious and merciful, slow to anger,
and of great kindness and repenteth Him of
the evil" (Joel ii. 13): despite of our many frail-
ties, shortcomings, and apostacies, ever "waiting
to be gracious!" You repeated the other night
in a few words what each one of us must feel ;
" double for all my sins :—double *mercy* I
mean." The Scripture account of the sinner
and the sinner's God is, " Our sins reach unto
the clouds ; " but, His mercy is *above* the clouds ;
it is high above the heavens. " The mercy of

the Lord is from everlasting to everlasting upon them that fear Him." I agree with you, we dare not measure God, or the mercy of God by any human standard. "With Him is plenteous redemption." "My thoughts are not your thoughts, neither are your ways My ways, saith the Lord." The beautiful name here given seems even to go a step further than mercy—"*Longsuffering.*" If He be so patient and longsuffering towards *us*, may we not well be patient and longsuffering towards Him and His dealings; bearing whatever He sees meet to lay upon us, specially when He lights the furnace, and subjects us to furnace-heat;—the "fiery trials" of your verse? Indeed may this not be His own way of leading to a heartier repentance? alike to deeper contrition for the past, and to quicken our longings for the future's better portion?

It is a precious text truly to meditate upon, sitting as it were under the portico of your loved Temple—"Behold the eye of the Lord is upon them that fear Him, upon them that *hope in His mercy*" (Ps. xxxiii. 18). You don't seem willing to forget the key-note in your last Easter Sermon—(or rather expounded Psalm)—"His mercy endureth for ever." That 'for ever' may well help—as it seems to do—to take your mind off present suffering. You comforted —— watching your distress and powerless to relieve you, when she simply remarked, "Heaven will make amends for all:"—you replied, "Oh yes, far more."

May I not add, it will *explain* all ? I have quite accidentally come on these lines which I may as well copy out. They recal our now almost-forgotten parable of the comet and its surrounding stars. The writer is speaking of the mystery of present grief and suffering: how the 'needs be' of these is often now concealed:—but that the time is coming when that 'needs be'

"Will flash before us out of life's dark night,
As stars shine most in deeper tints of blue;
And we shall see how all God's ways are right,
And how what seems reproof was Love most true.

But not to-day.   Then be content, poor heart!
HIS plans, like lilies pure and white unfold.
We must not tear the close-shut leaves apart,
Time will reveal the calyxes of gold,
And if through patient toil we reach the land
Where wearied feet with sandals loosed may rest,
Then we shall clearly own and understand—
                  God knew the best!"

Are you at this moment subjected to pain, I
much fear very severe pain?   It is from the
lips, remember, of a "longsuffering God," the
mandate and exhortation are addressed—

" *Beloved, think it not strange concerning the
fiery trial which is to try you, as though some
strange thing happened unto you."*

" After that ye have suffered awhile."

MY DEAR ——

We found this statement, in speaking of it together, to be full of comfort (1 Pet. v. 10).

It seems to say distinctly that all God's people may, in some form or other, expect trial or suffering. *" After that* YE *have suffered awhile."* " His fire is *in Zion,* and His furnace *in Jerusalem* " (Isa. xxxi. 9). It may perhaps be the very suffering to whose characteristics Peter here makes reference—that of the body. Have you not over and over again told me, that though subjected to other severe fatherly discipline; to physical pain, you have, during your life, been almost entirely a stranger ? It has come at last. And as you truly remarked (if I may expand what you said), many who dwell on the greater inten-

sity (and so far true) of mental anguish—
have perhaps never known the reality of what
you, and many other sufferers are now enduring: unfitting for work and duty: unfitting
very greatly for meditation and prayer: unfitting above all, as you added in words
never to be forgotten, for preparation to meet
God, if such preparation has been deferred till
the shadows are lengthening, and the final
darkness falling!   There can be, as you know
and have proved, many a soothing song in the
night of *bereavement*.   But these songs are
difficult to sing, when " the harp of a thou-
sand strings "—this sensitive bodily frame is
out of tune—or rather, when every nerve of
it becomes a chord of agony; in the morning
the cry ' Would God it were evening,' and in
the evening ' Would God it were morning!'

If such however be the too faithful experience in physical pain: these words of St.
Peter suggest the solacing thought, that the
sufferings of God's children have their assigned
limits—" *After that ye have suffered awhile!* "

In this as in other fiery trials, He Himself says, in a verse now very familiar—" I will afflict you *in measure.*" He will neither send us temptation nor suffering above that we are able to bear, but will, with the temptation, also make a way of escape that we may be able to bear it (1 Cor. x. 13).

And do not his words (taking all the verse together) further imply—and what you have so often expressed—that affliction is ever tempered with sweet and gracious alleviations? These in your case have been many, some over and above the ordinary ones. It may seem strange to single out what in its way is very subordinate to many others: but how soothing one of your former greatest pleasures has been to you! For I believe I am right in saying that no day during suffering weeks— with the drawing-room door open, so as to reach your couch of pain—have you failed to have these choicest of Christian hymns played and sung (as if preludes to the eternal song), beginning with " My faith looks up to Thee,"

ending at times with Mendelssohn's, " Oh, rest
in the Lord," or with the words, which ever
seem to sum up and epitomise all your longings—" Let me be with Thee where Thou art ! "
While speaking of hymns, I liked much what
you said (it may be a hint for others).   First
of all as to the consolation you yourself enjoy
during your sleepless hours in recalling and
repeating the well-known ones : but also, that
this very experience justifies the plan you
have followed, of getting your lads on Sunday
evenings to learn thoroughly by heart a *few* of
the choicer hymns and passages of Scripture
rather than many : coming over and over them
again, so as to impress them on their memories, and have thus a small but select store of
comfort ready for any similar hour of prostration overtaking !

But to come back to our verse of to-day :—
Well, surely, it is, that your sufferings,—the
existence of them, the *duration* of them, the
intensity of them, rest with this ' faithful God.'
Sorely tossed you still are on the waves of

tribulation, a "midnight sea." But the bark is not driven hither and thither by capricious winds. Not only does the Saviour come to you "in the fourth watch of the night," in the very midst of the storm, when the darkness is deepest, and whispers His own, "It is I;" but He enters the vessel and pilots it to the shore. Carrying out the figure, you can yet once more recall the comfort you have all along had in that passage: "So He brought them to the haven where they would be." That "so"—the 'while' of St. Peter's verse—is in safe and gracious hands. 'So,'—it may imply, through more waves, deeper darkness, cross currents, "breakers ahead." But each wave is narrowing the distance; bringing nearer heaven —nearer Home! You can say to Him whose "way is in the sea," in the words of a friend—

"Meantime along the darksome, billowy path
Thyself hast trod,
Lead, Saviour, lead me home in faith,
Home to my God,
To rest for ever after earthly strife,
In the calm light of everlasting life!"

Yes, looking forward from that "while"—
that "little while" here, to the glorious world,
where suffering in any form shall neither be
felt nor feared;—

*" Beloved, think it not strange concerning the
fiery trial which is to try you, as though some
strange thing happened unto you: but rejoice,
inasmuch as ye are partakers of Christ's sufferings; that, when His glory shall be revealed,
ye may be glad also with exceeding joy."*

Partakers of the Divine Nature.

MY DEAR ——

It is a wonderful height of glory and of bliss to which the words, which now offer themselves in turn to us, conduct. *" Partakers of the Divine nature"* ! (2 Pet. i. 4).

There is something even beyond what you dwelt so much upon last Sunday, in that beautiful picture in the seventh of Revelation, of God's tender hand wiping away, as it were, the last lingering tear-drops with which His sorely suffering people enter a tearless heaven. Your favourite figure of the stones in the Temple of Mercy, "living stones"— ever-living, *everlasting*—is more helpful to us here. In what way believers can be represented thus, as part and portion of that mystic Eternal Building, it is impossible to tell or to conceive. We took, you remember, the phrase

simply as an aid to thoughts and themes that
are in themselves *indescribable :* as one of the
' unspeakable ' words and visions referred to
in a former conversation, which St. Paul says
defy the powers and possibilities of human
language. Let us accept it in this its in-
describableness — " *Partakers of the Divine
nature*" *!* In the Church on earth, believers
are at times represented as stars and satel-
lites circling round the Great Sun of light and
love. Here they are spoken of as if blended
with that Sun—lost and swallowed up like
the exhaled dewdrop in the blaze of glory.
God Himself becomes ' all in all.' Even
your beautiful idea of the polished stones
seems in one sense to vanish, and be merged
in an emblem still more glorious. Well
surely may suffering be assuaged at least,
when confronted with such grandeur of everlasting hope as this ! I don't wonder at your
ceaseless ponderings of these kindred passages
in the prayer preceding the Saviour's Passion.
Peter, we have before surmised, may very pos-

sibly have heard that divine 'Intercessory.'
Who can tell but that the remembrance of it
may have even framed and suggested the present wondrous words? Let me recall them.
"That they all may be one as Thou Father
art in Me and I in Thee . . . and the glory
which Thou gavest Me I have given them!"
And *then*, the climax of the prayer, when the
promised glory is in the act of being revealed—
when, in your own case, present sufferings are
about to terminate and the earthly conflict to
cease: the hour of the spirit's release is liter-
ally an answer to that closing petition you so
love to have repeated—"Father, I will that
they also whom Thou hast given Me be with
Me where I am." Your last Sunday's remark
to —— was, 'How I long for the eternal Sabbath: pray that I may soon enjoy it!' That
prayer seems in all likelihood very shortly
to be answered. Your liking for Newton's
"Weary Traveller" is amply explained—

"Thus when the Christian Pilgrim views
By faith his mansion in the skies;

> The sight his fainting strength renews,
> And wings his speed to reach the prize."

These leaflet verses sent, seem even more appropriate than when first read to you, now that the weakness is so visibly increasing :—

> " Oh trust thyself to Jesus,
>   When flesh and heart do fail,
> And thou art called to enter
>   Death's dark o'ershadowed vale.
> Then is the hour for saying,
>   ' I will no evil fear ; '
> Then is the time for singing,
>   ' Lord—Thou art with me here.'
> O trust thyself to Jesus,
>   As thy spirit takes its flight
> From every earthly shadow,
>   To the land of perfect light.
> *Then* is the hour for saying,
>   ' Christ hath done all for me ; '
> Then is the time for singing—
>   ' *He* gives the *victory* ' ! "

Meanwhile, cleave to the " exceeding great and precious promises " spoken of in to-day's verse. They are represented there as ladder-steps, conducting to these heights of untold bliss. And as one after another is leading you ever

higher, upwards, heavenwards, homewards,—
let the Angels of the better than Bethel-
ladder—the Angels of covenant Promise and
Hope, whisper in your ear—

*" Beloved, think it not strange concerning the
fiery trial which is to try you, as though some
strange thing happened unto you: but rejoice,
inasmuch as ye are partakers of Christ's sufferings ; that, when His glory shall be revealed,
ye may be glad also with exceeding joy."*

Growth in Grace, and in the Knowledge of Jesus Christ.

MY DEAR ——

The last words of Peter's second epistle — his last message to a suffering church and a suffering world—come appropriately to mind to-day. " *Grow in grace and in the knowledge of our Lord and Saviour Jesus Christ* " (2 Pet. iii. 18).

It is worth noting, that as he began his two letters, so he concludes with, " *Our Lord and Saviour Jesus Christ,*"—Him who is " the First and the Last "—" the Author and Finisher of the Faith "—" the name that is above every name."

It is little else than farewell words also, to which *you* are now equal. Thank God you are able still, not only to *hear* them, but very recently at least to *give* them. I met the servants coming downstairs fresh from your room. I know you spoke, as your strength permitted you, faithful things to them (I saw from their tears how faithful they had been), and which they cannot fail to remember and treasure all their lives. I can guess the burden of what was said. Very much what Peter speaks of here as the one preparation for the solemn hour which sooner or later must overtake us all:—to ' grow in grace, and in the knowledge of Christ.'

The Apostle when he wrote these words, felt the nearness of his own summons—the coming of ' the day-dawn,' "Knowing that shortly I must put off this my tabernacle even as our Lord Jesus Christ hath showed me " (2 Pet. i. 14). None of all the disciples had so " grown in grace " as he had done. The once rash man was toned down, by the power of a divine spiritual force within him, to be meek and lowly and humble. Even with greater truth than " his beloved brother Paul " could he say—" By the grace

of God I am what I am." That same grace
doubtless quickened in him also this " knowledge " of his dear Lord. That loving Master
indeed was no longer with him as he had once
been, in bodily person. But the words of his
first epistle, he could now repeat with an ever-
increasing ardour—" Though now we see Him
not, yet believing, we rejoice with joy unspeakable and full of glory."

Suffering and trial had their own to do in
all this. Material helps they were in his spiritual progress, and in endearing to him the great
object of his faith. I know from your own
lips you have felt the same. These long weeks
have been like a chisel in God's hand polishing and preparing you for a place in the great
Temple; as you expressed it to———, "a precious
—most necessary discipline, that you could
not have wanted for anything." You remember
the thorn in the nest leading to upward
flight ? Has not your period of seclusion and
suffering, together, specially led you to grow
in " the knowledge " (and I may add *love*) " of

your Lord and Saviour " ? The old hymns you
ask for with an always new delight, are just
those which are fullest of the one cherished
theme. These two lines, memorable to you
and me from a sacred association, have sur-
vived all others—

> " How sweet the name of Jesus sounds
> In a believer's ear."

I can only find room to recall yet another
favourite thought with you (" and so much
the more as you see the day approaching ")—
that this knowledge will form the ever-in-
creasing joy of heaven:—the prayer of St.
Paul, the prayer and aspiration of eternity ;—
" that I *may* know Him." I have not forgotten what you have said about a sermon
you heard many years ago at G——g, on
'the object of life,'—" that I may win Him;"
and the one sentence in which you gave the
substance of it:—" If Christ be won, all is
won for this world and the next."

I am very sure you can add, " *This* is all
my salvation, this is all *my* desire!" Though

with failing voice, yet with increasing heart-emphasis, and that, despite of aches and sufferings, you can give to others your closing experience, even with the consciousness, too, that the last fiery trial cannot be far off—

" Beloved, think it not strange concerning the fiery trial which is to try you, as though some strange thing happened unto you: but rejoice, inasmuch as ye are partakers of Christ's sufferings; that, when His glory shall be revealed, ye may be glad also with exceeding joy."

Suffering according to the will of God.

MY DEAR ——

I do not wonder at your love for that verse of the Apostle—" *them that suffer according to the will of God* " (1 Pet. iv. 19), and that you yesterday asked specially to have sung to you—" Thy will be done." Let us be thankful for a little abatement of pain to-day. The shadow on the dial seems to have gone a trifle backward—at least for a time. We dare hope, I fear, no more: am I not right in adding, you wish no more? But that " shadow of the degrees "—as in the case of Hezekiah—is and has been entirely under the control of God. " Behold *I* will bring " (Isa. xxxviii. 8) were God's words to the sick and suffering king of Judah. The same comfort is Peter's here, and that of all subjected to bodily distress.

Were suffering—suffering such as yours—a chance or accidental occurrence, it would simply be unendurable. But the assurance that it is in accordance with *His* sovereign will, assuredly takes from it its acutest sting. " THOU hast known my soul in adversities." In entering on the first critical phase of this illness, your prayer was " Let me fall into the hands of God, for great are His mercies." And now, conscious of being in the same hands, and yet too surely anticipating a fatal result, you have been enabled in sweet submission to say—the Lord gave, and the Lord has a sovereign right to take away :—

" I only yield Thee what is Thine ! "

The same God who gave Jesus for you, has appointed the " fiery trial." After such a pledge of His love (I merely repeat what you have liked to hear over and over)—He can inflict no unnecessary pang. You remember the hymn of long long ago, which I know has been for years another of your early Sunday morning ones—

> " I cannot always trace the way
> Where Thou, Almighty One, dost move ;
> But I can always, always say
> That God is Love ! "

You yet once more expressed to me the old remark——" that your suffering is sore enough and hard enough to bear : but what would it be if you had been called to confront it without God and without hope——with a salvation and a Saviour still to seek ? " The thoughts suggested by to-day's verse, led you to add in some such words as these:——" What if I had even been called to its endurance with no settled conviction that it is the appointment of one too wise to err——too kind to be needlessly severe ? "

Thank God, you have not misjudged or misinterpreted His dealings;——the 'strangeness' of the " fiery trial." You have not so learned (or rather mislearned) the divine design and discipline. Though you said in your most suffering moments to —— to-day, " Oh, I hope it won't be long ! " I know that though ' a little longer' be the decree, it will be assented to

with a joyful "Even so, FATHER ! " *He* wills
it. There must be some infinite reason for the
prolongation, and that your earnest cry is yet
unsuccoured—"Make no tarrying, O my God!"
Seek to glorify Him, by continued trusting
Him in this mystery of anguish. Take the
completed words of St. Peter's verse: and,
conscious that you are thus 'suffering according to the will (or " by the appointment") of
God,' "*commit the keeping of your soul to
Him in well-doing.*" I have referred to Hezekiah. You remember how in his 'sore sickness,' " he turned his face toward the wall,
and *prayed unto the Lord.*" Further on, he
gives us one of the petitions of his prayer—
Is it not yours ?—"I am oppressed, under-
take for me ! " God has enabled you hitherto
to say, in the words of one whose " departure
was at hand," but who had none by him to
smooth his death-pillow—" I know whom I
have believed, and am persuaded that He is
able to keep that which I have committed
unto Him ! "

So you had, last night, ''Tis I'? Its soothing words seem never to weary you.

> [" Toss'd with rough winds, and faint with fear,
> Above the tempest, soft and clear,
> What still small accents greet mine ear?—
>   'Tis I ; be not afraid.
>
> 'Tis I, who washed thy spirit white ;
> 'Tis I, who gave the blind eyes sight ;
> 'Tis I, thy Lord, thy Life, thy Light ;
>   'Tis I ; be not afraid."]

Its middle verse comes with a special and specially needed support to you *now*—

> " Mine eyes are watching by thy bed,
> Mine arms are underneath thy head,
> My blessing is around thee shed ;
>   'Tis I ; be not afraid ! "

Yes, indeed, a beautiful soul-sustaining confidence,—Christ in the storm ; Christ appointing, and directing, and controlling, each wave in the pitchy darkness.   But in the midst of it all, with His own calm re-assuring word, rocking billow after billow to rest—"*It is I, be not afraid !*" Little did you think when you painted that big motto-board in your room—

["As thy days so shall thy strength be"]
—and hung it where it is, that it would be of so
much use to you :—not forgetting the two on
either side—" *To me to live is Christ,*" and " *To
die is gain.*" Shall I call it your own triplet
of consolation—very full and very precious ?

But I must stop ; for your favourite verses
and themes come crowding upon me, when I
think of you so low and so distressed : and I
know not which to ask you to dwell upon
more than another. Here, however, is one
which stands out very conspicuously. For I
have noted myself, and —— confirms me,
that with the single exception of what I call
your *great* verse, there is no one other which
during this long illness you have more frequently selected as your " night-thought to
sleep upon," or to muse upon when sleep was
impossible ; no one that seems to have raised
you so above your sufferings ;—" Fear not ; for
I have redeemed thee ; I have called thee by
thy name, thou art Mine ! " But I think I
may proceed with the quotation ; the words

which immediately follow seem the very ones you now require, and every hour their meaning will be more precious:—" When thou passest through the waters, I will be with thee; and through the rivers, they shall not overflow thee: when thou walkest through the fire, thou shall not be burnt; neither shall the flame kindle upon thee!"

With such an assurance from the lips of the very Being who is chastening you—

" Beloved, think it not strange concerning the fiery trial which is to try you, as though some strange thing happened unto you: but rejoice!"

The Coming of the Day of God.

My Dear ——

"The Day" is too surely soon to break, and the shadows—the shadows of pain and suffering and death—to flee away! "Watchman, what of the night—watchman, what of the night?" "The morning cometh." I know you are eagerly looking and longing for the Apostle's "day-dawn and day-star." Accordingly, though we were to search all Scripture, I do not think any verse could more thoroughly express your present feelings than the one which comes in order now—"*Looking for and hasting unto the coming of the day of God*" (2 Pet. iii. 12).

A week ago you were able, but then only very feebly, to speak of St. Peter's beautiful emblem here—ascending the mountain-height to catch the first faint blush of that eternal morning. No summons would to you be more joyous than this—" The Master is come and calleth for thee!" Do not think it was a selfish or impatient prayer: pain doubtless had its part in it, but it was something other and better than pain which yesterday prompted the cry—" Why tarry the wheels of His chariot?" The old Latin line will obtrude itself—

" Tendentemque manus, ripæ ulterioris amore !"

How pleased you were, when, after sleepless tossings, the early breeze entered your open window with the singing of birds, and when thanks were offered in prayer for the morning light and the return of day! You are now catching the faint but sure indications of a better dawn—" *the coming of the day of God :*" the day in which, to use words which are almost worn by repetition, for they have ever come to you like a strain of sweetest music— " And there shall be no more death, neither sorrow, nor crying, neither shall there be any more pain, for the former things are passed

away." I may add the companion verse—
"And He will swallow up death in victory;
and the Lord God will wipe away tears from
off all faces; . . . for the Lord hath spoken it"
(Isa. xxv. 8). Cling resolutely, in the midst
of present darkness, to the assurance that your
night of tempest will—must—erelong have
its ending, and *then*, "the rest shall be glorious"! Let me remind you of the account
of St. Paul's shipwreck:—"They cast four
anchors out of the stern and *wished for the day.*"
. . . And so "it came to pass that they escaped
all safe to land" (Acts xxvii. 29, 44).

Meanwhile, let patience have its perfect
work. "God's time," as some old writer says,
"is well worth the waiting for." What you
quoted to me a few evenings ago, in a very
different sense as matter of encouragement to
another, you may apply to yourself and your
attitude of submission to the divine will—

"They also serve who only stand and wait."

"All the days of my appointed time will I

wait, until my change come." " I wait for the Lord, my soul doth wait, and in His word do I hope. My soul waiteth for the Lord more than they that watch for the morning: I say, more than they that watch for the morning." If all seems too surely to indicate that that waiting time cannot be deferred :—to the ever more earnest prayer, " Make haste, my Beloved!"—your once suffering but now glorified Saviour has the answer ready—" And when these things begin to come to pass, then look up, and lift up your heads; for your redemption draweth nigh " (Luke xxi. 28). Redeemed from sin: redeemed from suffering: redeemed from death. Shall I recall to you your own words, two nights ago, when, to lessen the darkness, I thought I had managed, unobserved, to introduce another candle outside your door ? — " And there shall be no night there ! "

I shall try, as you ask, to see your friend's impressive picture [that of a soul entering Heaven]. I think you said it represented an

K

embodied spirit passing through a vista of
angels to receive the crown from the Saviour's
hands: and that the *Great* Figure was indi-
cated alone by a blaze of glory. That very
vision is now yours; and the reality will soon
be still more your own. We all know what
the central point of your mental picture is.
It was expressed in the reply last evening to
——'s question, ' What hymn shall be sung
at prayers?' "*Safe in the arms of Jesus.*"
You are now passing—(the text you heard at
R——) passing through "the swellings of
Jordan." But it is with the old promise,
" When thou passest through the waters I
will be with thee!" We have, jotted down
in your own handwriting, the comforting
and appropriate words of another — "Our
friends can only go with us to the brink of
the dark river, but Jesus can carry us safely
through."

" The morning now is breaking,
　The night will soon be o'er:
I am kneeling on the threshold;
　My hand is on the door.

I am longing for the Master
To bid me rise and come,
To the glory of His presence,
To the gladness of His Home ! "

With the bright anticipation of " the new Heavens and the new earth " spoken of immediately following our verse of to-day (2 Pet. iii. 13)—the Everlasting arms underneath you now, and around you for ever !—

" *Beloved, think it not strange concerning the fiery trial which is to try you, as though some strange thing happened unto you : but rejoice, inasmuch as ye are partakers of Christ's sufferings ; that, when His glory shall be revealed, ye may be glad also with exceeding joy.*"

The Abundant Entrance.

————

I cannot adopt again the familiar form. You are beyond the reach of pen and voice now. You have finally emerged from "the fiery trial," reached "the haven where you would be." The polishing of the stone for Mercy's Temple is completed; the longing cry has been heard and answered—"*Let me go, for the day breaketh !*" The verse so oft sung, and which at last could only be silently listened to, has had its prayer graciously ful-filled—

> " When ends life's transient dream ;
> When death's cold sullen stream
>   Shall o'er me roll :
> Blest Saviour, then in love,
> Fear and distrust remove,
> O bear me safe above—
>   A ransomed soul ! "

When a loved friend pointed to the card

with the words upon it—" PERFECT THROUGH
SUFFERING," you replied, " Not yet ! " When
the same friend added—' Complete in Him:
perfect through His righteousness ' ; you bowed
your head and said—" Yes ! " Now, in that
" clothing of wrought gold "—" without fault
before the throne," you have the longing desire of your heart realised,—" with Christ,
which is far better." We can turn the words
of promise which appropriately occur to-day
into a glorious reality :—only we must change
the future tense into the past—" *So an entrance*
HAS BEEN *ministered unto you abundantly into
the everlasting kingdom of our Lord and Saviour
Jesus Christ*" (2 Pet. i. 11). His ineffable
glory, the glory of His immediate presence
and love *has* been revealed, and you are " *glad
also with exceeding joy.*" ' We shall soon meet
again,'—' I wish we could all go together,'
was your expressed and only unfulfilled desire. The battle was long and severe : thank
God I speak alone of the physical conflict.
But the victory now is sure. It is, without

doubt, an " abundant entrance." The *long* affliction will seem to you now " the *light* affliction which was but for a moment" (2 Cor. iv. 17). The verse in Isaiah we frequently read and meditated on together— with its varied emblems of suffering, seemed sadly realised in your experience, " floods," " rivers," " fires," " flames " (many, diversified, severe). But the words with which these emblems are ushered in, quoted and pondered equally often during these trying weeks;— words which had from your earliest years an earthly, have now an eternal heavenly significance—" I have redeemed thee, I have called thee by thy name, thou art Mine !" If I have spoken of the terribleness of the final struggle, glorious at least were the last articulate utterances—That *soliloquy* (if I may appropriately call it so) will not readily be forgotten—" Sweet rest! sweet rest! sweet rest! which remaineth for the people of God!" You have entered it now; and the words shall have a place on the tombstone

which loving hands and hearts will rear.
Christ became increasingly precious to you.
When the shadows of that 'long long dark
Valley' were falling ever thicker; when consciousness and utterance were so rapidly failing, that the presence and voice of those most
dear were scarce recognisable—

> " Not heralded by fire and storm,
>   In shadowy outline dimly seen,
> Came through the gloom a glorious Form,
>   The Living—Loving Nazarene ! "

The last, but oft-repeated word was the sum
and centre of your peace, and joy, and hope—
" Jesus," " Jesus," " Jesus!"—and one yet more
assured testimony—" Safe in the arms of
Jesus ! " All unknown, you had ofttimes, on
Sabbath evening, sung the hymn-prayer that
was thus to be so marvellously answered—

> " Till then I would Thy love proclaim
>   With every fleeting breath,
> *And may the music of Thy name*
>   *Refresh my soul in death.*"

As you were thus receding in the valley-
gloom, rather leaving those behind you there,

—yourself nearing the "glorious light"— what more could we wish for than this? It was like the assuring announcement, the signal waved on the other side of Jordan, the last echoes of the voice of suffering sounding over the tumultuous billows: it was the first and glorious utterance of Heaven as you passed through your favourite ' Gate of Pearl,'—" Safe in the arms of Jesus!" Shall I call it, too, the farewell word left behind you to weeping mourners and beloved friends? a word *for* them, as well as *to* them;—the closing reminder of the one grand end which through a consistent life you had often sought for others—and in some cases with brave fidelity pressed on others; it was befitting to tell aloud as your final testimony, ere your voice was blending with ministering seraphim,—" *Safe in the arms of Jesus!* "

" The last *enemy* that shall be destroyed is Death."

" O GIVE THANKS UNTO THE LORD, FOR HE IS GOOD: FOR HIS MERCY ENDURETH FOR EVER.

Let the redeemed of the Lord say so, whom He hath redeemed from the hand of the enemy."

Once more,—and let this be the concluding sentence which the pen of affection and of gratitude traces in these tribute-pages. Among other lowly legacies of faith and prayer and godly influence, this specially precious one has been, above all others, bequeathed to the children of weariness and pain and sore suffering. It survives your hour of departure, so that being dead you may yet speak. It comes floating down in the soft whisper of heaven's love as if an echo from within the veil—

" Beloved, think it not strange concerning the fiery trial which is to try you, as though some strange thing happened unto you : but rejoice, inasmuch as ye are partakers of Christ's sufferings ; that, when His glory shall be revealed, ye may be glad also with exceeding joy."

" Let me go ! the Day is breaking ! "
· Christ and His salvation taking :
Christ my only portion making :
Every other trust forsaking.
In the hope of life partaking,
In the bliss of Heaven upwaking,—
" Let me go ! the Day is breaking ! "

"WHEREFORE, BELOVED,

SEEING YE LOOK FOR SUCH THINGS,

BE DILIGENT,

THAT YE MAY BE FOUND OF HIM IN PEACE

WITHOUT SPOT AND BLAMELESS."

(*St. Peter's 2d Epistle* iii. 14.)

GLEAMS

FOR

THE SICK CHAMBER:

Being Daily Texts for a Month, suited for

the Sick and Suffering.

SUPPLEMENTARY.

The preceding part of this Book contains " Gleams from the Sick Chamber." The writer has thought it might make the Volume more available for the use of those for whom it is intended, to append some " Gleams for the Sick Chamber";—a series of appropriate Scripture verses for each day of the month (morning and evening), many of which have their sacred associations with the previous pages. All, conversant with beds of pain, know well, that there are often cases where the physical strength is unequal for any further effort than listening to a single text at a time. The selection which follows may also prove silent helps and comforts to the 'Weepers and Watchers' of the sick chamber, as well as the sufferers.

*** *Still further to adapt them for the end in view, these texts have been issued along with this Book (and may be had of the Publishers), in the form of a Roll in large type.*

I.

THE LOVED ONE SICK.

Morning.

"Lord, behold, he whom Thou lovest is sick." JOHN xi. 3.

Evening.

"And Jesus went about . . . healing all manner of sickness." MATTHEW iv. 23.

———◊———

II.

THE GIVER OF THE SICK CUP.

Morning.

"What shall I say? He hath both spoken unto me, and Himself hath done it." ISAIAH xxxviii. 15.

Evening.

. "The cup which my Father hath given me, shall I not drink it?" JOHN xviii. 12.

III.

THE GREAT PHYSICIAN AND HIS BALM.

𝔐orning.

"Is there no balm in Gilead? Is there no Physician there?"   JEREMIAH viii. 22.

𝔈bening.

"I am the Lord that healeth thee."

EXODUS xv.

———

IV.

A PILLOW FOR THE SICK-BED.

𝔐orning.

"The Lord will strengthen him upon the bed of languishing: Thou wilt make all his bed in his sickness."   PSALM xli. 3.

𝔈bening.

"Therefore I will look unto the LORD; I will wait for the God of my salvation: my God will hear me."   MICAH vii. 7.

V.

THE STILL HOUR.

𝕸orning.

" Commune with your own heart upon your bed, and be still." PSALM iv. 4.

𝔈bening.

" I was dumb, I opened not my mouth, because Thou didst it." PSALM xxxix. 9.

———◦———

VI.

WHY SICKNESS AND SUFFERING.

𝕸orning.

" This sickness is . . . for the glory of God, that the Son of God might be glorified thereby." JOHN xi. 4.

𝔈bening.

" Now no chastening for the present seemeth to be joyous, but grievous: nevertheless afterward it yieldeth the peaceable fruit of righteousness unto them which are exercised thereby." HEBREWS xi. 11.

VII.

A GENTLE KNOCK AT THE SICK CHAMBER.

𝔐orning.

" Behold, I stand at the door, and knock: if any man hear My voice, and open the door, I will come in to him, and will sup with him, and he with Me." Rev. iii. 20.

𝔈bening.

" Come in, thou blessed of the Lord wherefore standest thou without ? "

Gen. xxiv. 31.

VIII.

THE BEST OPIATE.

𝔐orning.

" Even so, Father ! for so it seemed good in Thy sight." Matt. xi. 26.

𝔈bening.

" Come unto Me, all ye that labour and are heavy-laden, and I will give you rest."

Matt. xi. 28.

IX.

PATIENT SUFFERING AND THE PATIENT SUFFERER.

Morning.

"For ye have need of patience, that, after ye have done the will of God, ye might receive the promise." HEB. x. 36.

Evening.

"Consider HIM . . . lest ye be wearied and faint in your minds." HEB. xii. 3.

X.

A PILLOW FOR THE DAY AND FOR THE NIGHT.

Morning.

"When I awake I am still with Thee." Ps. cxxxix. 18.

Evening.

"In the night his song shall be with me, and my prayer unto the God of my life." Ps. xlii. 8.

L

XI.

SWEETEST SOLACES.

Morning.

"Like as a father pitieth his children."

Ps. ciii. 13.

Evening.

"As one whom his mother comforteth, so will I comfort you; and ye shall be comforted."

Isa. lxvi. 13.

XII.

THE CANDLE LIGHTED.

Morning.

"Thou wilt light my candle the Lord my God will enlighten my darkness."

Ps. xviii. 28.

Evening.

"Thy right hand shall hold me. If I say, Surely the darkness shall cover me; even the night shall be light about me."

Ps. cxxxix. 10, 11.

XIII.

A PRESCRIPTION AND PROMISE.

Morning.

" Rest in the Lord, and wait patiently for Him." Ps. xxxvii. 7.

Evening.

" My grace is sufficient for thee : for my strength is made perfect in weakness."
2 Cor. xii. 9.

———

XIV.

SICK-BED ALLEVIATIONS.

Morning.

" I will sing of mercy and judgment."
Ps. ci. 1.

Evening.

" He stayeth His rough wind in the day of the East wind." Isa. xxvii. 8.

XV.

THE GREAT SYMPATHISER.

𝔐orning.

" We have not an high priest which cannot be touched with the feeling of our infirmities; but was in all points tempted like as we are, yet without sin." Heb. iv. 15.

𝔈bening.

" Himself took our infirmities, and bare our sicknesses." Matt. viii. 17.

———◦———

XVI.

A MEAN OF RESTORATION.

𝔐orning.

" And the prayer of faith shall save the sick." James v. 15.

𝔈bening.

" In the day of my trouble I will call upon Thee: for Thou wilt answer me."

Ps. lxxxvi. 7.

XVII.

THE SLEEPLESS WATCHER.

Morning.

"He that keepeth thee will not slumber."

Ps. cxxi. 3.

Evening.

"Behold, He that keepeth Israel shall neither slumber nor sleep." Ps. cxxi. 4.

XVIII.

TWO ANODYNES.

Morning.

"For He doth not afflict willingly, nor grieve the children of men." Lam. iii. 33.

Evening.

"I know, O Lord, that Thy judgments are right, and that Thou in faithfulness hast afflicted me." Ps cxix. 75.

XIX.

THE PAINLESS WORLD.

Morning.

"The inhabitant shall not say, I am sick."   Isa. xxxiii. 24.

Evening!

"Neither shall there be any more pain ; for the former things are passed away."

Rev. xxi. 4.

———o———

XX.

FEVER-THIRST QUENCHED.

Morning.

"My soul thirsteth for God, for the living God."   Ps. xlii. 2.

Evening.

"I will give unto him that is athirst of the fountain of the water of life freely."

Rev. xxi. 6.

XXI.

A WHISPER IN THE EAR OF THE SICK ONE, AND ITS ANSWER.

Morning.

"Is it well with thee?   It is well."

2 Kings iv. 26.

Ebening.

"The Lord direct your hearts into the love of God, and into the patient waiting for Christ."   2 Thess. iii. 5.

— o —

XXII.

THE NIGHT-WATCHES.

Morning.

"I remember Thee upon my bed, and meditate on Thee in the night-watches."

Ps. lxiii. 6.

Ebening.

"God, my Maker, who giveth songs in the night."   Job xxxv. 10.

XXIII.

THE PILLOW MADE SMOOTHER

𝔐orning.

"As thy days, so shall thy strength be."

Deut. xxxiii. 25.

𝔈bening.

"Commit thy way unto the Lord; trust also in Him; and He shall bring it to pass."   Ps. xxxvii. 5.

—o—

XXIV.

NO CURE IMPOSSIBLE.

𝔐orning.

"Behold, the Lord's hand is not shortened, that it cannot save; neither His ear heavy, that it cannot hear."   Isa. lix. 1.

𝔈bening.

"Is anything too hard for the Lord?"

Gen. xviii. 14.

XXV.

A SUFFERER'S SOLILOQUY.

Morning.

" Why art thou cast down, O my soul ?
and why art thou disquieted in me ? "

Ps. xlii. 5.

Evening.

" Hope thou in God : for I shall yet
praise Him, who is the health of my countenance, and my God."   Ps. xlii. 11.

—*o*—

XXVI.

A GREATER SUFFERER.

Morning.

" Christ also suffered for us."   1 Pet. ii. 21.

Evening.

" Behold, and see if there be any sorrow
like unto my sorrow ! "   Lam. i. 12.

XXVII.

THE SHADOW ON THE DIAL.

Morning.

" Behold, I will bring again the shadow of the degrees, which is gone down in the sun-dial, ten degrees backward."

Isa. xxxviii. 8.

Evening.

" So wilt Thou recover me, and make me to live."   Isa. xxxviii. 16.

XXVIII.

THE LIFE-VOW.

Morning.

" Because He hath inclined His ear unto me, therefore will I call upon Him as long as I live."   Ps. cxvi. 2.

Evening.

" The living, the living, he shall praise Thee, as I do this day."   Isa. xxxviii. 19.

XXIX.

LIFE OR DEATH.

𝕸orning.

"To me to live is Christ, and to die is gain." PHIL. i. 21.

𝕰vening.

"For whether we live, we live unto the Lord; and whether we die, we die unto the Lord: whether we live therefore, or die, we are the Lord's." ROM. xiv. 8.

———o———

XXX.

WAITING.

𝕸orning.

"All the days of my appointed time will I wait, till my change come." JOB xiv. 14.

𝕰vening.

"Wait on the Lord; be of good courage, and He shall strengthen thine heart: wait, I say, on the Lord." PS. xxvii. 14.

XXXI.

NUNC DIMITTIS.

Morning.

"To depart and be with Christ, which is far better."   PHIL. i. 23.

Evening.

"Lord, now lettest Thou Thy servant depart in peace, according to Thy word: for mine eyes have seen Thy salvation."

LUKE ii. 29, 30.

———◇———

" To

HIM

BE GLORY BOTH NOW

AND EVER.

AMEN."

(*Concluding words of St. Peter's Epistles.*)

 PRINTED BY BALLANTYNE, HANSON AND CO.
EDINBURGH AND LONDON.

Printed in the United States
153983LV00009B/40/A